11+ MATHS
REVISION GUIDE

David E Hanson

Published by Galore Park Publishing Ltd
19/21 Sayers Lane, Tenterden, Kent TN30 6BW
www.galorepark.co.uk

Text copyright © David E Hanson 2012

Cover design by Helen Boosey
Design by Qué, Wittersham
Typesetting by Typetechnique
Technical illustrations by Ian Moores Graphics

Printed by Charlesworth Press

ISBN 978 1 905735 761

First published 2012, reprinted 2013

Details of other Galore Park publications are available at www.galorepark.co.uk

Acknowledgements

I would like to thank the reviewers of my early manuscript for their constructive suggestions, the
team at Galore Park for helping to make the book happen and especially Caitlin Grant for her
valuable assistance at all stages in the preparation of this book.

David E Hanson

CONTENTS

2 Throughout the book, page numbers which are prime numbers are coloured orange instead of black. See if you can learn them all!

INTRODUCTION

This book has been written to help you revise. It is designed to remind you rather than teach you.

Throughout, you are encouraged to
- look at things in different ways
- look for patterns
- ask questions – 'What if …?', 'How …?', 'When …?'

In each chapter you will find
- **explanations** of important ideas
- **questions**, including
  - traditional questions, requiring written or drawn answers
  - multiple choice questions
- **things to do**, which could include
  - practical tasks
  - investigations
  - challenges
  - games to play
  - using real-life occasions for 'painless' practice
- **top tips** to help you remember key information
- **aim high** material, which is more challenging, to help stretch and develop your skills further.

The syllabus and examinations

Examination syllabuses, such as those for the ISEB 11+ and the Kent Test, are based upon
- the Programme of Study for Key Stage 2 of the National Curriculum, and
- the Framework for the National Numeracy Strategy up to, and including, Year 6.

Syllabuses are revised from time to time and it is important to be aware of the latest arrangements.

For completeness, and for the interest of high achievers, a little of the material covered in this book may be just outside the requirements of the current syllabus.

It is also a good idea to
- obtain copies of recent past papers
- find out about any expectations or requirements of a target school.

Note Questions follow the ISEB syllabus format and are numbered either:

1.   (a)
     (b)
     (c)   where parts of questions are not related

OR

1.   (i)
     (ii)
     (iii)   where parts of questions are related

A note for teachers

This book has been written primarily for parents to use with their children. It should not, in any way, conflict with the good groundwork done in schools. Some of the ideas may be presented in ways which are different from those normally found in textbooks. The intention here is to stimulate a little lateral thinking in young minds, in the hope that this might increase understanding and encourage resourcefulness.

A note for parents

This book has been written primarily to assist the increasing number of parents who wish to support their children in preparation for the important assessment and selection process at 11+.

Many parents

- are unsure of what may need to be done and how best to help
- cannot remember the maths they did at school
- believe that they are 'no good at maths'
- are anxious about helping their own children.

All parents want the best for their children.

Some children

- have not discovered the fun that maths can offer
- have not fully mastered the basics, and therefore feel that they are 'no good at maths'
- think that maths is 'for school' and are reluctant to do maths at home
- are embarrassed or worried at the prospect of being helped by their own parents.

It is a good idea to discuss any concerns with teachers. Teachers may feel, with justification, that parental intervention is unnecessary and a wise parent will respect a teacher's judgement. Even if this is the case, there are plenty of 'fun' activities which can be tackled by children and parents together. The **things to do** are particularly useful here.

It is certainly important for parents to familiarise themselves with the relevant knowledge, skills and understanding, so that help can be provided if this should prove to be necessary.

It should be emphasised that parental support should be

- pleasurable for all concerned – maths can be, and *should* be, fun!
- provided at a time when there are no rival attractions or distractions, or when tiredness could be a factor
- totally stress free.

How to use this book

It is suggested that you

- read through the text which **explains** the important ideas. Even if you consider that all is well in a particular section, it is a good idea to ask yourself questions such as 'What if …?', 'How …?', 'When …?' It really helps to look at things in different ways
- answer the **questions**, which are designed to be completed on your own – answers to the questions are at the back of the book
- tackle the **things to do**, many of which are more fun if you can do them with friends, your parents or other adults
- take note of the **top tips** and **aim high** material, especially if you want to improve and develop your skills.

On page 156, Appendix 2, you will find 'Programming in BBC Basic' which is a fun way to use a computer to help with basic mathematical skills. Try it and see the fun you can have!

[W] Downloadable worksheets are available where graphs or grids are required for some questions. These are available from www.galorepark.co.uk

Tips on revising

It is suggested that you should

- get physical exercise, such as going for a walk, before revising
- eat healthy food, such as fresh fruit, whilst revising
- appreciate that you know, understand and can do a great deal already, so keep calm and don't worry
- set yourself a realistic target, such as concentrating just on 'Shape'
- work for a short time, such as 15 minutes, and then take a break before continuing
- have a good night's sleep.

Tips on the final preparation for an exam

You will have worked on past papers so you will know roughly what to expect with the examination paper.

You will already have some experience of examinations, so you know what it feels like. We are all different, but most people will be apprehensive.

Assuming that you have worked hard in class and you have revised thoroughly, you will be in a good position to do your best.

It is suggested that you

- make sure you have everything you need, such as pens, pencils and drawing instruments, checked and ready in good time (at the latest, the day before)
- get a good night's sleep so you can think clearly in the exam
- eat a sensible breakfast so you do not feel hungry during the exam
- resist the temptation to do any last minute revision
- keep calm
- take a small bottle of water into the exam, if this is allowed
- make sure that you go to the lavatory and wash your hands before you enter the exam room.

Avoid

- leaving everything until the last minute
- rushing about, getting hot and sweaty
- doing anything which might affect your eyes, such as going for a swim or giving the cat a hug!

Tips on what to do in an exam

It is suggested that you

- listen to, and read, all instructions very carefully
- read each question very carefully, remembering that a single word, such as 'not', can change a question considerably
- work as quickly and as neatly as you can
- show all your working and/or give full explanations, remembering that, in many cases, showing what you are doing is more important than just getting the right answer!
- check that your answers are sensible and complete
- don't worry, or spend a lot of time, if there is something you can't remember or do – just leave it and come back to it after you have done everything else.

USEFUL RESOURCES

From the same series: *11+ English Revision Guide* by Susan Hamlyn, ISBN 9781905735587

Study Skills by Elizabeth Holtom, ISBN 9781902984599

Mixed Maths Exercises Pupil's Book: Year 6 by Andrew Jeffrey, ISBN 9780903627030
Mixed Maths Exercises Answers: Year 6 (download) by Andrew Jeffrey, code D0322004
Mathematics Questions at 11+ (Year 6) Book A Questions by David E Hanson, ISBN 9780903627092
Mathematics Questions at 11+ (Year 6) Book A: Answers by David E Hanson, ISBN 9781907047152
Mathematics Questions at 11+ (Year 6) Book B Questions by David E Hanson, ISBN 9780903627351
Mathematics Questions at 11+ (Year 6) Book B: Answers by David E Hanson, ISBN 9781907047145

Junior Maths Book 1 by David Hillard, ISBN 9781905735211
Junior Maths Book 1 Answer Book by David Hillard, ISBN 9781905735228
Junior Maths Book 2 by David Hillard, ISBN 9781905735235
Junior Maths Book 2 Answer Book by David Hillard, ISBN 9781905735242
Junior Maths Book 3 by David Hillard, ISBN 9781905735266
Junior Maths Book 3 Answer Book by David Hillard, ISBN 9781905735297

So you really want to learn Maths Book 1 by Serena Alexander, ISBN 9781902984186
So you really want to learn Maths Book 1 Answer Book by Serena Alexander, ISBN 9781902984193
So you really want to learn Maths Book 2 by Serena Alexander, ISBN 9781902984315
So you really want to learn Maths Book 2 Answer Book by Serena Alexander, ISBN 9781902984322

Galore Park is sole distributor of the Independent Schools Examinations Board (ISEB) past papers for Common Entrance examinations and Common Academic Scholarship Examinations

All this plus much more available from Galore Park: www.galorepark.co.uk

1 NUMBER

Can you imagine a world without numbers? Numbers are everywhere – on your watch and mobile phone, on the pages in your book and even on your shoes! Numbers are an important part of everyday life. Numbers in themselves are very interesting, but it is what you can do with them that is really exciting!

1.1 PROPERTIES OF NUMBERS

Types of number

Whole numbers

Whole numbers (integers) can be

- **positive** | EXAMPLES: 3, 48, 10 000 |

  These could be written $^+3$, $^+48$ and so on but most of the numbers we use are positive so we leave out the positive signs.

- **negative** | EXAMPLES: $^-2$, $^-13$, $^-50$ |

  Negative numbers are sometimes, inappropriately, called 'minus' numbers. Negative numbers are used when we describe temperatures below zero.

Positive and negative numbers are sometimes referred to as **directed numbers**.

Integers are used when

- **counting (cardinal** numbers) | EXAMPLES: 1, 2, 3, 4, … |

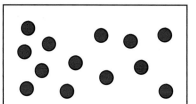

  There are 13 circles in the rectangle.

  Cardinal numbers are always positive.

- **ordering (ordinal** numbers) | EXAMPLES: 1st, 2nd, 3rd, 4th, … |

  Ordinal numbers can show a position on a number line and can be positive or negative.

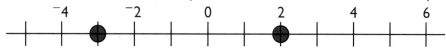

  The positions $^-3$ (negative 3) and 2 are marked on this number line.

  John won a silver medal for finishing 2nd in the 100 metre race.

- **naming**

  A famous soccer player always wears a shirt bearing the number 7

Fractions

Fractions can be

- **proper** | EXAMPLES: $\frac{1}{2}, \frac{2}{3}, \frac{11}{20}$

Proper fractions describe the number of parts out of a whole. The **denominator** (bottom number) is the number of parts in the whole and the **numerator** (top number) tells us how many of those parts we are considering. In a proper fraction the numerator is smaller than the denominator.

This square has 4 parts and 3 of them are shaded. $\frac{3}{4}$ (three quarters) of the whole square is shaded.

- **improper** | EXAMPLES: $\frac{3}{2}, \frac{4}{3}, \frac{11}{4}$

In an improper fraction we have more parts than would make one whole. The numerator is larger than the denominator.

This diagram shows the improper fraction $\frac{5}{4}$ (five quarters).

- **mixed** | EXAMPLES: $1\frac{1}{4}, 1\frac{1}{3}, 2\frac{3}{4}$

In a mixed fraction we have a whole number part and a proper fraction part.

Mixed fractions can be changed into improper fractions, and vice versa.

This diagram shows the mixed fraction $1\frac{1}{4}$ (one whole and a quarter of a whole).

Decimals

EXAMPLES: 1.4, 3.08, 0.2

Decimals are used in

- **measures** | EXAMPLE: 3.8 centimetres

- **money** | EXAMPLE: £6.45

COFFEE	£1.23
STEAK	£6.45
LEMONADE	£0.90

Percentages

EXAMPLE: 50%

A **percentage** is the number of parts out of 100

We will look at fractions, decimals and percentages in more detail in section 1.4

The language of the four basic number operations

Addition

● The **sum** of 3 and 6 is 9 $3 + 6 = 9$

● 3 **plus** 6 is 9

● Other words associated with **addition** include: total, more, together, and, added to, increased, greater, up.

● With addition, the order of the numbers does not matter. We say that the operation is **commutative**.

> EXAMPLES:
> $6 + 3 = 9$ and $3 + 6 = 9$
> $^-6 + 3 = ^-3$ and $3 + ^-6 = ^-3$
> $^-6 + ^-3 = ^-9$ and $^-3 + ^-6 = ^-9$

AIM HIGH

Subtraction

● The **difference** between 4 and 12 is 8 $12 - 4 = 8$

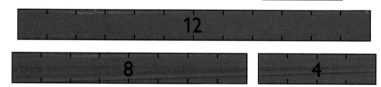

● To find the difference we always take the smaller number from the larger number so the difference is always positive.

● 12 **minus** 4 is 8

● 4 **subtracted from** 12 is 8

● Other words associated with **subtraction** include: less, take away, fewer, lower, down, from.

● With subtraction, the order of the numbers *does* matter. We say that the operation is *not commutative*.

> EXAMPLES:
> $6 - 3 = 3$ but $3 - 6 = ^-3$
> $^-6 - 3 = ^-9$ but $3 - ^-6 = 9$
> $^-6 - ^-3 = ^-3$ but $^-3 - ^-6 = 3$

AIM HIGH

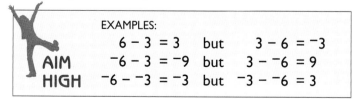

TOP TIP

It is very important to make the distinction between ⁻2 (negative 2) and – 2 (minus 2). Negative 2 is a number below zero and can stand alone. Minus 2 is an operation and cannot stand alone. Minus 2 has meaning only when we say what we are taking 2 away from, for example
$8 - 2$

- Note that there is a difference between the **minus** sign (the operation subtraction, linking two numbers, as in 6 − 3) and the **negative** sign (the state of being below zero, applied to a single number, as in ⁻3).

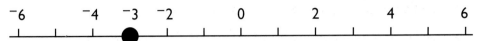

On the number line above, the position of the number ⁻3 is shown.

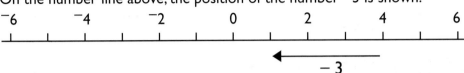

On the number line above, you can see what happens when we subtract 3 from 4

- Subtracting 3 is an **operation**; ⁻3 is a **number**.

Multiplication

- The product of 3 and 12 is 36 | $3 \times 12 = 36$ |

- 3 **times** 12 is 36

- 12 **multiplied by** 3 is 36

- Other words associated with **multiplication** include: lots of, groups of, rows of.

- With multiplication, the order of the numbers does not matter. Multiplication is **commutative**.

$3 \times 4 = 12$

$4 \times 3 = 12$

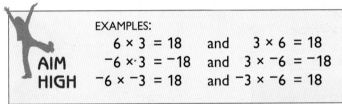

EXAMPLES:
$$6 \times 3 = 18 \quad \text{and} \quad 3 \times 6 = 18$$
$$^-6 \times 3 = ^-18 \quad \text{and} \quad 3 \times ^-6 = ^-18$$
$$^-6 \times ^-3 = 18 \quad \text{and} \quad ^-3 \times ^-6 = 18$$

AIM
HIGH

Spinners 1

Make three spinners with regular decagons cut from stiff card, as shown (right).

Number each spinner 0, 1, 2, 3, 4, 5, 6, 7, 8, 9. Spin the spinners and note the numbers on which they come to rest. Multiply any two of the numbers and add the third. What are the smallest and the largest numbers which you could make?

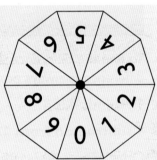

Spinners 2

Using the same spinners, is there any number less than 90 which you could *not* make? How many different ways could you make 10, 50 and 80?

Division

- The **dividend** divided by the **divisor** gives the **quotient**.

- Words associated with **division** include: goes into, shared, split equally.

- With division, the order of the numbers *does* matter. We say that the operation is **not commutative**.

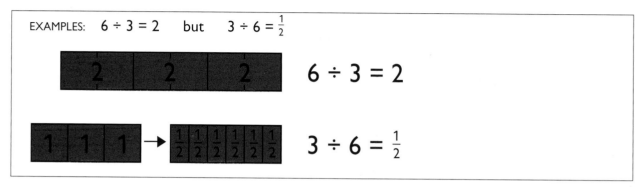

EXAMPLES: $6 \div 3 = 2$ but $3 \div 6 = \frac{1}{2}$

$6 \div 3 = 2$

$3 \div 6 = \frac{1}{2}$

- 6 divided by 3 is 2 $\boxed{6 \div 3 = 2}$

- 6 sweets **shared** between 3 people gives them 2 sweets each.

- 3 divided by 6 is $\frac{1}{2}$

- 3 pizzas shared by 6 people gives them $\frac{1}{2}$ a pizza each.

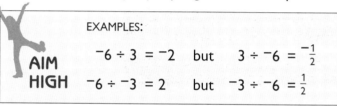

EXAMPLES:

$^-6 \div 3 = {}^-2$ but $3 \div {}^-6 = \frac{^-1}{2}$

$^-6 \div {}^-3 = 2$ but $^-3 \div {}^-6 = \frac{1}{2}$

- If a division is not exact, then we get a **remainder**.

EXAMPLES:

$5 \div 3 \rightarrow 1$ remainder 2

$13 \div 4 \rightarrow 3$ remainder 1

remainder 1

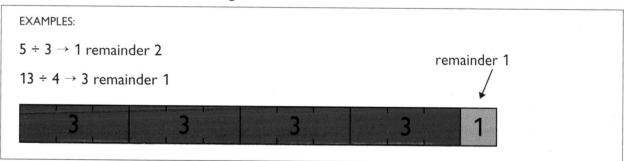

Note that here we have chosen to use an arrow (to mean 'gives' or 'leads to') rather than an equals sign.

We will look at the four basic operations in greater detail in section 2.1

Even numbers and odd numbers

Even numbers

- End in 0, 2, 4, 6 or 8
- Can be divided by 2, so all even numbers are **multiples** of 2

Odd numbers

- End in 1, 3, 5, 7 or 9
- When divided by 2 always give the **remainder** 1

There are useful '**rules**' concerning operations with **even numbers** and **odd numbers**.

Operation	even + even	even + odd	odd + even	odd + odd
+	even e.g. 2 + 2 = 4	odd e.g. 4 + 3 = 7	odd e.g. 5 + 4 = 9	even e.g. 7 + 5 = 12

Operation	even − even	even − odd	odd − even	odd − odd
−	even e.g. 6 − 4 = 2	odd e.g. 8 − 3 = 5	odd e.g. 9 − 2 = 7	even e.g. 7 − 3 = 4

Operation	even × even	even × odd	odd × even	odd × odd
×	even e.g. 2 × 4 = 8	even e.g. 4 × 3 = 12	even e.g. 5 × 4 = 20	odd e.g. 7 × 9 = 63

Operation	even ÷ even	even ÷ odd	odd ÷ even	odd ÷ odd
÷ (if the result is an integer)	depends on the numbers e.g. 6 ÷ 2 = 3 (odd) 8 ÷ 2 = 4 (even)	even e.g. 12 ÷ 3 = 4	gives remainder 1 only even numbers can be divided exactly by an even number	odd e.g. 35 ÷ 7 = 5

Counting on and counting back

We can count on or back in steps of any size.

EXAMPLE 1:
1, 5, 9, 13, 17, ….
counting on, from 1, in steps of 4

EXAMPLE 2:
12, 14.5, 17, 19.5, 22, ….
counting on, from 12, in steps of 2.5

EXAMPLE 3:
100, 93, 86, 79, 72, ….
counting back, from 100, in steps of 7

EXAMPLE 4:
10, 7, 4, 1, ⁻2, ⁻5, ….
counting back, from 10, in steps of 3

 TOP TIP

Can you be 'counted on' to 'count on' accurately? When counting on and counting back, it is useful to think of patterns. Notice that in Example 1 the numbers are all odd and in Example 3 the numbers are even and odd alternately.

Questions

The answers are at the back of the book.

1.1 Tom and Jerry each thought of a positive integer less than 10

When they add the two numbers the result is an even number.

The difference between the two numbers is also an even number.

The product of the two numbers is an odd number.

When they divide Tom's number by Jerry's number, the result is Jerry's number.

(i)   What is Jerry's number?   (2)

(ii) What type of number is Tom's number?   (1)

(iii) What is
    (a) the sum   (1)
    (b) the difference   (1)
    (c) the product   (1)
    for the two numbers?

1.2 Copy and complete the following:

(i) $7 + 4 =$ (1)

(ii) $8 - 5 =$ (1)

(iii) $7 \times 4 =$ (1)

(iv) $12 \div 6 =$ (1)

(v) $^-4 + {}^-5 =$ (1)

(vi) $5 - {}^-4 =$ (1)

(vii) $^-3 \times 2 =$ (1)

(viii) $12 \div 5 \rightarrow$ (1)

1.3 James keeps a record of the temperatures inside and outside his window at midday.

(i)   On 1 June the temperature outside was 24 °C and the temperature inside was 7 degrees lower. What was the inside temperature?   (1)

(ii) On 1 January the temperature outside was $^-4$ °C and the temperature inside was 19 degrees higher. What was the temperature inside?   (2)

Sequences

● A **sequence** is an ordered group of numbers which follows a 'rule'.

● The individual numbers in the sequence are the **terms** of the sequence.

EXAMPLE 1: 1, 5, 9, 13, 17, ….	The rule for finding the next term is 'add 4'.
EXAMPLE 2: 100, 95, 90, 85, 80, ….	The rule is 'subtract 5'.

In addition to the simple 'counting on' or 'counting back' rules, we can have sequences which follow more interesting rules!

EXAMPLE 3: 1, 3, 9, 27, 81, ….	The rule is 'multiply by 3'.
EXAMPLE 4: 40, 20, 10, 5, ….	The rule is 'divide by 2'.
EXAMPLE 5: 1, 2, 3, 5, 8, ….	The rule is 'add the last two terms'.

Number chains

Choose a number less than 100

If the number is even, divide it by 2

If the number is odd, add 3

Follow the same instructions on the result to form a chain of numbers.

EXAMPLES: 15 → 18 → 9 → 12 → 6 → 3 → 6 → 3 → ....

Stop when you start going round in circles!

16 → 8 → 4 → 2 → 1 → 4 → 2 → 1 → ....

Investigate. See what you can discover!

What would happen if, instead of adding 3, you added 5 or 7?

Questions

The answers are at the back of the book.

1.4 Copy these 'counting on' or 'counting back' sequences and write the next three terms of each one.

(i)	1, 6, 11, 16, 21, ...	(1)
(ii)	47, 40, 33, 26, 19, ...	(2)
(iii)	4.0, 4.2, 4.4, 4.6, 4.8, ...	(2)

1.5 Write the next two numbers in these sequences.

(i)	11	19	27	35	43	....	(1)
(ii)	100	93	86	79	72	....	(1)
(iii)	15	12	9	6	3	....	(2)

1.6 Write the next two numbers in these sequences.

(i)	2	3	5	8	13	....	(2)
(ii)	1	4	9	16	25	....	(1)
(iii)	2	8	18	32	50	....	(2)

Digits

- 5 is a **single-digit** number – where 5 is the units digit.

- 17 is a **two-digit** number – where 7 is the units digit and 1 is the tens digit.

- 342 is a **three-digit number** – where 2 is the units digit, 4 is the tens digit and 3 is the hundreds digit.

- An **abacus**, like the one on the right, can be useful in understanding this.

- You will notice that there is a 'spike' for the units, a spike for the tens and so on. Each spike has space for 9 beads.

- If we start with an empty abacus, and count, placing beads on the units spike, to represent the numbers 1, 2, 3, 4 and so on, we can get up to 9 on the units spike.

- To represent 10, we put one bead (representing one 10) on the tens spike and remove all the beads from the units spike.

- To continue counting, we put beads on the units spike again until we reach 19

Th	H	T	U
	3	4	2

You may have noticed that the abacus shown above has a horizontal line drawn above 4 beads. Don't worry about this now. There is a reason for this which will be explained in section 1.3

We will look at abacuses in more detail in section 1.2

More number chains

Choose any two-digit number.

Double the units digit and then add the tens digit

Follow the same instructions on the result to form a chain of numbers.

EXAMPLES: 15 → 11 → 3

Stop when you reach a single-digit number.

99 → 27 → 16 → 13 → 7
37 → 17 → 15 → 11 → 3

Do this a number of times and see what you can discover!

Multiples

A **multiple** of a number 'n' is a number which can be divided exactly by 'n'.

> EXAMPLE:
> The multiples of 5 are 5, 10, 15, 20, 25, 30, …. and so on.
> Notice that 5 is counted as a multiple of itself.

- Multiples of 5 end in either 5 or 0

- Multiples of 2 are even and end in 0, 2, 4, 6, or 8

- When a multiple of 4 is divided by 2, the result is even.

- Multiples of 3 are numbers which divide by 3 and include 3, 6, 9, 12, 15, ….

- Multiples of 6 are even and also divide by 3

TOP TIP

If you add the digits in a multiple of 3, then the total of the digits is divisible by 3 e.g. we know that 432 is a multiple of 3 because (4 + 3 + 2) = 9 and 9 divides by 3

Number square

On a copy of this number square shade in all multiples of 3 and circle all multiples of 5

0	1	2	3	4	5	6	7	8	9
10	11	12	13	14	15	16	17	18	19
20	21	22	23	24	25	26	27	28	29
30	31	32	33	34	35	36	37	38	39
40	41	42	43	44	45	46	47	48	49
50	51	52	53	54	55	56	57	58	59
60	61	62	63	64	65	66	67	68	69
70	71	72	73	74	75	76	77	78	79
80	81	82	83	84	85	86	87	88	89
90	91	92	93	94	95	96	97	98	99

What patterns can you see?

What can you say about the numbers which are both shaded and circled?

On a new copy of the number square, shade in the multiples of two other numbers and look for other patterns.

Multiplication tables

- The **multiples** of a number can be set out in a **table**, like the **two times** table below.

1	2	3	4	5	6	7	8	9	10	11	12
2	4	6	8	10	12	14	16	18	20	22	24

- Thorough understanding and knowledge of multiplication tables, at least up to ten times, is extremely important, as is the ability to recall, quickly and accurately, the individual multiplication facts.

- Some people find this very daunting but a multiplication table 'square' can be used as a safety check until you feel more confident.

1	2	3	4	5	6	7	8	9	10	11	12
2	4	6	8	10	12	14	16	18	20	22	24
3	6	9	12	15	18	21	24	27	30	33	36
4	8	12	16	20	24	28	32	36	40	44	48
5	10	15	20	25	30	35	40	45	50	55	60
6	12	18	24	30	36	42	48	54	60	66	72
7	14	21	28	35	42	49	56	63	70	77	84
8	16	24	32	40	48	56	64	72	80	88	96
9	18	27	36	45	54	63	72	81	90	99	108
10	20	30	40	50	60	70	80	90	100	110	120
11	22	33	44	55	66	77	88	99	110	121	132
12	24	36	48	60	72	84	96	108	120	132	144

TOP TIP

The dark shaded squares show the multiplication facts which are often hardest to learn.

AIM HIGH

It is a good idea to practise your understanding of this table frequently until you are confident.

You will notice that

- the table is **symmetrical** about the shaded diagonal

- the shaded diagonal shows the **square numbers** 2 × 2, 3 × 3, 4 × 4 and so on

- there are **patterns** in the multiples of a particular number – for example, in the nine times table, the units digit goes down 1 and the tens digit goes up 1 as you move from one multiple to the next.

- There are relatively few **multiplication facts** which may be harder to learn.

- These are dark shaded on the table and there are only six of them!

- Remember that 6 × 9 is the same as 9 × 6 and it often helps to 'switch the numbers round'.

- As with all of the tables, 'practice makes perfect'!

The table on page 10 is much more than a multiplication table!

It is also a very useful **division table**.

- Look at division by 7

- For 56 divided by 7 you
  - look along the 7 times row until you reach 56
  - look up the column to find that 7 × 8 is 56, so 56 divided by 7 is 8

- For 40 divided by 7 you
  - look along the 7 times row until you reach 40 or a number which is close to 40 as 40 is not there
  - notice that 35 (7 × 5) and 42 (7 × 6) are there
  - realise that 7 will not 'go into' 40 six times
  - decide that 7 will go into 40 five times, with **remainder** 5 (40 − 35).

> **TOP TIP**
>
> If there are one or two multiplication facts which prove difficult to learn, write them on colourful card and put the cards in frequently seen places such as on the fridge door, above the TV, on the back of your mobile phone or on a mirror.

Common multiples

- 56 is a multiple of 7 and a multiple of 8, since it is in both the 7 times table and the 8 times table.

- We say that 56 is a **common multiple** of 7 and 8

Factors

- 7 is a **factor** of 56 because 7 divides *exactly* into 56

- 8 is also a factor of 56

- 7 and 8 form a **factor pair** of 56, because they multiply together to make 56

Factor 'rainbows'

7 and 8 are not the only factors of 56

● For any number, we can draw a **factor rainbow** which shows all of the pairs of factors.

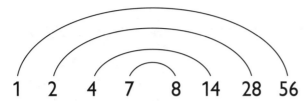

1   2   4   7   8   14   28   56

The factor rainbow for 56 has four arcs because there are four factor pairs:

1 × 56   2 × 28   4 × 14   7 × 8

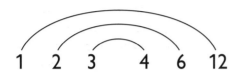

1   2   3   4   6   12

The factor rainbow for 12 has three arcs because there are three factor pairs:

1 × 12   2 × 6   3 × 4

● We can represent 12 in six ways as **factor strips**:

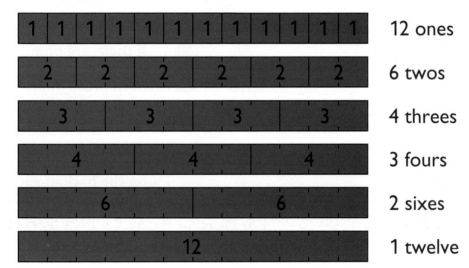

1 1 1 1 1 1 1 1 1 1 1 1	12 ones
2 2 2 2 2 2	6 twos
3 3 3 3	4 threes
4 4 4	3 fours
6 6	2 sixes
12	1 twelve

Prime numbers

For a **prime number**, the factor rainbow has only one arc.

EXAMPLES:

1   7   1   13   7 and 13 are prime numbers.

● Prime numbers do not appear in the 'body' of the multiplication table on page 10.

● As a factor strip, a prime number can be represented in only two ways.

1 1 1 1 1 1 1   7 ones   7   1 seven

1 1 1 1 1 1 1 1 1 1 1 1 1   13 ones

13   1 thirteen

● A prime number has no factors except 1 and itself.

The prime numbers below 100 are:

2	3	5	7	11	13	17	19	23	29
31	37	41	43	47	53	59	61	67	71
73	79	83	89	97					

TOP TIP

If you bid on eBay, then bidding always in prime numbers of pounds and pence (for example £7.23) is a very good way of learning, and remembering, the prime numbers.

Note that

- 1 is *not* a prime number

- 2 is the *only even* prime number

- none of these numbers appears in the body of the multiplication table.

Prime factors

The **prime factors** of a number are the factors which are prime numbers.

EXAMPLE 1:
The prime factors of 12 are 2 and 3
We can write 12 as 2 × 2 × 3

EXAMPLE 2:
The prime factors of 56 are 2 and 7
We can write 56 as 2 × 2 × 2 × 7

- Every integer can be written as a product of its prime factors.

EXAMPLES:

20 = 2 × 2 × 5   21 = 3 × 7   22 = 2 × 11   23 = 23 (prime)

24 = 2 × 2 × 2 × 3   25 = 5 × 5 (square)   26 = 2 × 13   27 = 3 × 3 × 3 (cube)

- We can find the prime factors of a number by dividing by the prime numbers, as many times as possible, in order of increasing size.

EXAMPLES:

2	24
2	12
2	6
3	3
	1

so 24 = 2 × 2 × 2 × 3

2	20
2	10
5	5
	1

and 20 = 2 × 2 × 5

Factor trees

A **factor tree** may be drawn for any number which is not a prime number.

EXAMPLES:

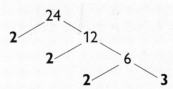

Compare the factor trees with the division method above.

Square numbers

The **square numbers** appear in the diagonal of the multiplication table (see page 10).

- The square of a number is the number multiplied by itself.

> EXAMPLE 1:
> The square number 64 is the square of 8 because $8 \times 8 \rightarrow 64$
>
> EXAMPLE 2:
> The square number 121 is the square of 11 because $11 \times 11 \rightarrow 121$

TOP TIP

An arrow (→) is sometimes used instead of the equals sign (=) to mean 'gives' rather than 'is equal to'.

- We can write this as $n \times n \rightarrow n^2$

- We say that n^2 is 'the square of n', or 'n squared'.

- In the factor rainbow of a square number, the 'inside' loop joins a number to itself.

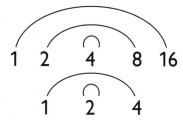 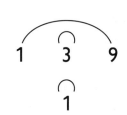

- For a square number, *one* of its factor strips can be drawn as n strips of n.

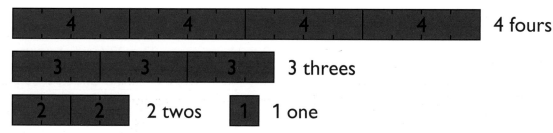

4 fours

3 threes

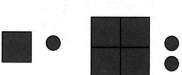 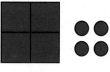 2 twos   1 one

- Note that 1 is a square number.

- Square numbers can also be represented as patterns of squares or dots where the number of rows is the same as the number of columns.

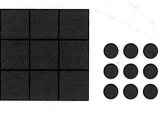 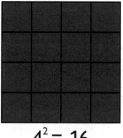 

$1^2 = 1$ $2^2 = 4$ $3^2 = 9$ $4^2 = 16$

- The first 20 square numbers are:

1	4	9	16	25	36	49	64	81	100
121	144	169	196	225	256	289	324	361	400

- We can write 2×2 in shorthand as 2^2 which we say as 'two squared'.

- The little raised number, ^{2}, is an **index number**.

> **AIM HIGH**
>
> Look what happens when we subtract **consecutive** square numbers.
>
> $16 - 9 \rightarrow 7$ $25 - 16 \rightarrow 9$ $36 - 25 \rightarrow 11$ and so on.
>
> Can you see a pattern?

Square roots

The **square root** of an integer is the number which when multiplied by itself will give the integer.

> EXAMPLE 1: The square root of 4, written in shorthand as √4, is 2 because 2 × 2 → 4
>
> EXAMPLE 2: The square root of 169, √169, is 13 because 13 × 13 → 169

In the two examples above, the square roots are integers because 4 and 169 are both square numbers.

AIM HIGH

EXAMPLE 3: The square root of 12 is not so straightforward because 12 is not a square number.

- Look again at the factor rainbow for 12

- There is no 'middle' number which arcs to itself.   1   2   3   4   6   12

- The nearest arc links 3 and 4 so you might expect that the square root of 12 lies somewhere between 3 and 4

- The square of 3 is 9 (3 less than 12) and the square of 4 is 16 (4 more than 12) so it seems reasonable to think that the square root of 12 would be about half way between 3 and 4 and slightly nearer to 3 than to 4

- 3.5 is half way between 3 and 4 and, when it is worked out, √12 is approximately 3.46

Cube numbers

AIM HIGH

Cube numbers (often simply called **cubes**) can be represented by models made from little cubes.

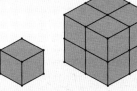 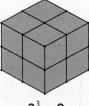 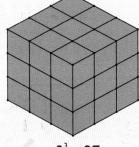 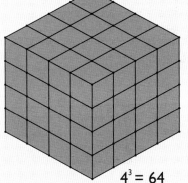

$1^3 = 1$ $2^3 = 8$ $3^3 = 27$ $4^3 = 64$

- The first five cube numbers are:

  1   8   27   64   125

- The cube of a number n can be written $n \times n \times n$ which in shorthand is n^3 where the little ^{3} is an index number.

Spinners 3

Invent a game to play with your friends or parents using the three spinners you used for Spinners 1 and 2 (see page 4). For example, you could score 10 points for a square number, 20 points for a cube number and for a prime number you could add the prime number to your score!

Lotto results

The table below shows the *Lotto Plus 5* results for a week in July.

Day/date							Bonus
Sun 10	12	14	18	27	31	32	25
Mon 11	18	31	36	39	41	43	2
Tue 12	1	12	22	24	29	36	26
Thu 14	1	2	32	34	38	41	5
Fri 15	4	8	22	31	32	44	41

(i) If prime numbers are counted as they are, square numbers count for 10 points, cube numbers count for 20 points and a bonus number score is doubled, which day would give the greatest score?

(ii) Make a note of the *Lotto Plus 5* results every week, with each friend or family member choosing a day beforehand. See who gets the highest score.

Cube roots

AIM
HIGH

- The cube root of 8 is 2 because $2 \times 2 \times 2 = 8$
- We can write this as $\sqrt[3]{8} \rightarrow 2$ where the symbol $\sqrt[3]{}$ indicates the cube root.

Number game

For this game, you will need

- a copy of the number square on page 10, or a number track, 1 metre long, numbered 0 to 99 (a metre rule [available in wallpaper shops] or a measuring tape would be fine)
- two ordinary dice
- a small counter, such as a button, for each player.

You may like to make up your own rules for the game, but here are some suggestions to get you started.

On the number square, shade all prime numbers red, all square numbers blue and all cube numbers yellow.

Roll the two dice and find the

- sum
- difference, or
- product

of the numbers and move forward that number of places.

If you land on

- a prime number, move on to the next prime number
- a square number, move back to the previous square number
- a cube number, go back to the start at zero!

You will soon be able to remember the prime, square and cube numbers.

Questions

The answers are at the back of the book.

1.7 (a) Draw a factor rainbow for 48 (4)

(b) List all of the factor pairs for 18 (2)

1.8 Here are some number cards.

| 4 | 5 | 11 | 12 | 15 | 24 | 27 | 33 | 35 |

Choose from the numbers above

(i) a multiple of 7 (1)

(ii) a factor of 10 (1)

(iii) a square number (1)

(iv) all the prime numbers (2)

(v) the number which can be written as $2 \times 2 \times 2 \times 3$ (1)

(vi) the number which is a common multiple of 3 and 5 (1)

(vii) two numbers which have a product of 48 (1)

(viii) two numbers which have a difference of 9 (1)

(ix) three numbers which have a sum of 55 (2)

(x) a cube number (1)

Multiple choice questions

In these questions you should write the letter of the correct answer.

1.9 How many of the following numbers are even? (1)

8 13 25 40 59 66 71 87 92 108
A: 3 B: 4 C: 5 D: 6 E: 7

1.10 Which of these pairs of numbers has the largest difference? (1)

A: 43 − 19 B: 94 − 67 C: 91 − 63 D: 53 − 26 E: 82 − 55

1.11 How many of these numbers are prime? (1)

1 2 3 19 27 49 63 79 91 111
A: 3 B: 4 C: 5 D: 6 E: 7

1.12 In how many of these calculations does the symbol ✳ represent 13? (1)

7 + ✳ = 20   31 − ✳ = 19   24 − 11 = ✳
9 + ✳ = 22   3 × ✳ = 39   28 + ✳ = 41
A: 2 B: 3 C: 4 D: 5 E: 6

1.13 Which of these has the smallest sum? (1)

A: 3 + 2 B: 7 + ⁻5 C: ⁻1 + 3 D: 3 + ⁻4 E: 2 + ⁻1

1.14 If you count back from 100 in 4s, which of these numbers will you **not** reach? (1)

A: 96 B: 88 C: 72 D: 54 E : 12

1.15 How many of these numbers are multiples of 3? (1)

18 45 54 65 78 102 123 666 900 10 101
A: 5 B: 6 C: 7 D: 8 E: 9

1.2 PLACE VALUE AND ORDERING

Reading and writing numbers

- The number shown on the abacus (right) is read 'two thousand, nine hundred and twenty'.

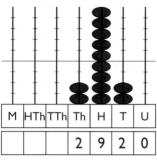

M	HTh	TTh	Th	H	T	U
			2	9	2	0

- Similarly the number 40 705, (shown right), is read 'forty thousand, seven hundred and five'.

- The number thirteen thousand and eleven is 13 011 when written in figures.

M	HTh	TTh	Th	H	T	U
		4	0	7	0	5

Place value

In the numbers 2920, 40 705 and 13 011, the zeros are very important in keeping the **place value** of the digits.

This is particularly important when we are

- multiplying or dividing a number by 10, 100 or 1000

and when we are

- comparing

- ordering

- rounding (see section 1.3)

numbers.

TTh	Th	H	T	U
	2	9	2	0
4	0	7	0	5
1	3	0	1	1

Questions

The answers are at the back of the book.

1.16 (i) Write in numerals (figures) the number six thousand and twenty.   (1)

   (ii) Write in words the number 40 404   (1)

1.17 The value of the 8 in 3805 is 800 (8 hundreds).

   (i) What is the value of the 5 in 1350?   (1)

   (ii) What is the value of the 9 in 129 345?   (1)

   (iii) In the number 4601.6 how many times greater is the value of the 6 on the left than the 6 on the right?   (2)

1.18 Put a decimal point in each of these numbers so that the 7 has the value of 7 tenths.

   437   8971   75   (3)

Multiplying a number by 10, 100 or 1000

- When we multiply a number by 10, we simply move the digits one place to the left, as shown in the abacus pictures below.

$$308 \times 10 = 3080$$

TTh	Th	H	T	U
		3	0	8
3	0	8	0	

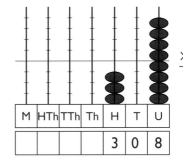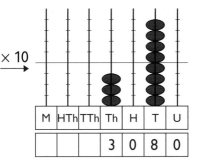

- When we multiply a number by 100 we move the digits two places to the left.

$$53 \times 100 = 5300$$

TTh	Th	H	T	U
			5	3
5	3	0	0	

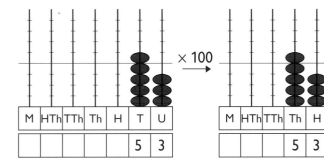

- We follow the same rules with decimals, as shown in the example below where 4.09 is multiplied by 100 to give 409

$$4.09 \times 100 = 409$$

H	T	U .	t	h	th
		4 .	0	9	
4	0	9			

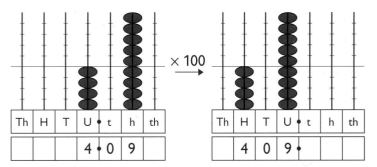

- We always fill any 'empty' places on the *right*, up to and including the units place, with zeros, as in the first two examples above.

TOP TIP

When multiplying decimals, some people prefer to 'move the point' rather than 'move the digits'.

Dividing a number by 10, 100 or 1000

● Dividing a number by 10 works in the same way, but this time we move the digits one place to the right.

30.8 ÷ 10 = 3.08

H	T	U	.	t	h	th
3	0	.	8			
	3	.	0	8		

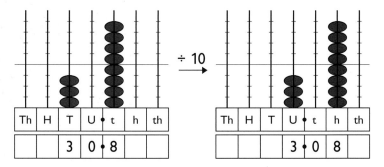

● When we divide a number by 100, we move the digits two places to the right.

6.7 ÷ 100 = 0.067

H	T	U	.	t	h	th
	6	.	7			
	0	.	0	6	7	

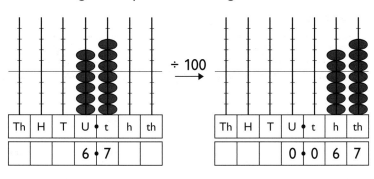

● This time we fill any 'empty' spaces on the left, up to and including the units place, with zeros.

Sliding abacus

Make your own sliding abacus. This can be used to demonstrate what happens when a number is multiplied, or divided, by 10, 100 or 1000.

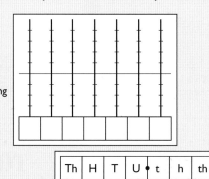

slide 2 places
←
when multiplying by 100

Make it from paper or thin card using the downloadable master. Cut the abacus into two pieces as shown in the diagram above.

If the pieces are laminated, you can draw beads with a marker pen and then wipe them off when you have finished, so that you can re-use the abacus.

Who wants to be a millionaire?

Make a spinner like the one shown below.

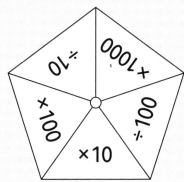

Play a game with your friends. Start off with an imaginary one pound coin each. Take it in turns to spin the spinner and keep a record on paper of how much 'money' you have.

EXAMPLE:

Tina		Caitlin		Mandy	
Spin	**New amount (£)**	**Spin**	**New amount (£)**	**Spin**	**New amount (£)**
start	1	start	1	start	1
×10	10	×100	100	÷10	0.1
÷100	0.1	×10	1000	×100	10

The winner is the first person to reach a million pounds. Anyone who finishes up with less than one penny is out of the game!

Questions

The answers are at the back of the book.

1.19 (i) Multiply 406 by 100 (1)

(ii) Divide 30.5 by 10 (1)

(iii) Multiply 2.95 by 10 (1)

(iv) Divide 3040 by 100 (1)

(v) Multiply 0.0305 by 100 (1)

1.20 (i) How many times more than 456 is 45 600? (1)

(ii) How many times more than 7.14 is 7140? (1)

(iii) How many times more than 0.05 is 500? (1)

(iv) How many times more than 7.4 is 7400? (1)

(v) How many times more than 1.09 is 109 000? (1)

Comparing numbers

When you **compare** two or more numbers, think of abacus pictures or write them one above the other in place value columns.

EXAMPLE: comparing the numbers 99, 1002 and 305

- On an abacus, 99 will need 18 beads, 305 will need 8 beads and 1002 will need only 3 beads.

Th	H	T	U
		9	9
1	0	0	2
	3	0	5

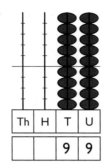
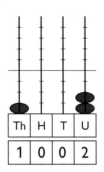
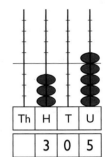

- The size of the digits is not as important as the place value of the digits.

AIM HIGH

It is the same idea with decimals. The place value of a digit is more important than its size.

EXAMPLE: comparing 0.078, 3.04, 0.506

U	t	h	th
0 . 0		7	8
3 . 0		4	
0 . 5		0	6

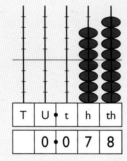
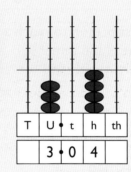
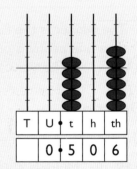

Ordering numbers

When we write a group of numbers in order of **increasing**, or **decreasing**, size, think about the place value of the digits.

EXAMPLE: ordering 987, 1789, 879, 978 and 798

- You need to look at the most **significant** digit first.

- In the list above, the numbers all have three digits apart from 1789 where the 1 represents a thousand.

- This is the most significant digit.

You can draw or imagine an abacus to help you to understand.

Th	H	T	U
	9	8	7
1	7	8	9
	8	7	9
	9	7	8
	7	9	8

In order of increasing size, the above numbers are:

Th	H	T	U
	7	9	8
	8	7	9
	9	7	8
	9	8	7
1	7	8	9

To do

Three-digit numbers

Make a set of number cards 1 to 9

| 1 | 2 | 3 | 4 | 5 | 6 | 7 | 8 | 9 |

Choose any three cards.

Arrange the three cards to make **six** different three-digit numbers.

For example, the cards:

| 4 | 6 | 9 |

give us the numbers 469, 496 and so on.

Write the six numbers down and then write them in order of increasing size.

The number line

A number line can be very useful when we are **comparing** or **ordering** numbers.

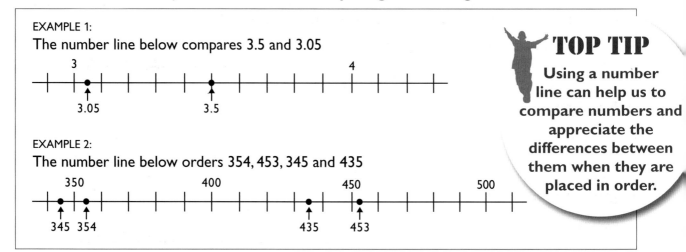

EXAMPLE 1:
The number line below compares 3.5 and 3.05

EXAMPLE 2:
The number line below orders 354, 453, 345 and 435

TOP TIP

Using a number line can help us to compare numbers and appreciate the differences between them when they are placed in order.

To do

Comparing numbers on a number line

The table below shows the lowest recorded temperatures (rounded to the nearest degree Celsius) in various countries and at the South Pole.

	Temperature in °C
Nepal	$^-45$
England	$^-26$
Philippines	$^+2$
Greece	$^-28$
Israel	$^-14$
Singapore	$^+19$
Mexico	$^-32$
South Pole	$^-82$

Record these as labelled dots on a copy of the number line below.

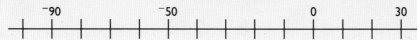

Using signs

We can use the **equal to** sign (=) when the numbers on each side have the same value.

EXAMPLE 1: $2 + 3 = 5$

We can also use the equals sign when we know that a number x has a particular value.

EXAMPLE 2: $x = 2$

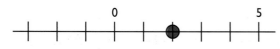

Other useful signs are:

- **greater than (>)**

EXAMPLE: $x > 2$ represents an unknown number larger than 2

We can represent this on a number line.

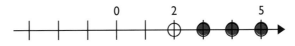

- **less than (<)**

EXAMPLE: $x < 4$

- **greater than or equal to (≥)**

EXAMPLE: $x \geq {}^{-}3$

- **less than or equal to (≤)**

EXAMPLE: $x \leq 5$

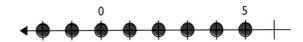

Larger or smaller game

This game can be played by 2, 3, 4 or 6 players. Using a set of nine number cards (as in the 'To do' on page 23), choose any four cards.

Now prepare a new set of cards, each card with one of the 24 (yes 24!) different four-digit numbers which can be made from the four numbers.

It may help if you make an organised list of the four-digit numbers in order of increasing size.

EXAMPLE:

| 3456 | 3465 | 3546 | and so on.

Rules of the game

- Shuffle the 24 cards with four-digit numbers and deal them out. You don't need to use all the cards.

- Keep all the cards hidden.

- Roll a die to decide who starts.

- Players take turns to put down a larger number than the last one.

- If a player 'can't go' then the turn is missed.

- When no-one has a higher number, then the rule switches to playing a lower number.

- Continue until no-one has a lower card and then switch back to playing a higher number.

- The first player to 'get rid of' all their cards is the winner.

The game is not as simple as it may seem and some clever tactics can be employed! Playing your highest higher card may, or may not, be the best move.

You could also try five-digit numbers. How many five-digit number cards would you make?

Questions

The answers are at the back of the book.

1.21 (i) On the number line below, the number ⁻4 is shown as a black dot.

Copy the number line. Mark clearly with a cross (X) the number which is 9 more than ⁻4 (1)

(ii) On a copy of the number line below, mark clearly with a cross the number which is exactly half way between ⁻0.6 and 1.8 (1)

(iii) On a copy of the number line below, mark clearly with a cross the mixed fraction $2\frac{1}{4}$ (1)

$$
\begin{array}{cccccc}
0 & 1 & 2 & 3 & 4 & 5
\end{array}
$$

1.22 (i) On a copy of the number line below, mark clearly all the integers x such that $x < 2$ (2)

$$
\begin{array}{ccc}
^-5 & 0 & 5
\end{array}
$$

(ii) On a copy of the number line below, mark clearly all the integers y such that $y \geq {}^-1$ (2)

$$
\begin{array}{ccc}
^-5 & 0 & 5
\end{array}
$$

1.23 (i) Write these numbers in order of *increasing* size.

769   697   796   679   967 (2)

(ii) Write these numbers in order of *decreasing* size.

3.45   4.53   3.54   5.34   4.35 (2)

Multiple choice questions

In these questions you should write the letter of the correct answer.

1.24 When these numbers are arranged in order of increasing size, which one is in the middle? (1)

A: **678**   B: **867**   C: **768**   D: **687**   E: **786**

1.25 Which number is exactly half way between 28 and 44? (1)

A: **32**   B: **34**   C: **35**   D: **36**   E: **38**

1.26 Which of these calculations gives the largest result? (1)

A: **305 × 100**

B: **3.05 × 1000**

C: **3 050 000 ÷ 10 000**

D: **0.305 × 10 000**

E: **30 500 ÷ 10**

1.3 ESTIMATION AND APPROXIMATION

Estimation

We can estimate

- a **number of objects**

> EXAMPLE: Estimate (do not count) the number of dots in the rectangle below.
>
>
>
> - You can use different strategies when making estimates.
>
> - A strategy here might be to make a rough count of the number of dots in an imaginary centimetre square and then multiply this by a guess at the number of square centimetres in the rectangle.
>
> - You might guess that there are **approximately** (about) 8 dots in a typical centimetre square and that the rectangle has an area of approximately 10 square centimetres.
>
> - This would give an estimated number of dots in the rectangle as 80
>
> - If you now count the dots, you will find that there are 78, so the estimate is fairly accurate.

TOP TIP

An estimate is only approximate. It is a rounded number.

How many?

Estimate the number of dried peas in a jar or the number of 1 penny coins you could fit onto a sheet of A4 paper.

When estimating a large number of things, it is important to be able to explain your answer rather than just taking a wild guess.

We can estimate

- the **result of a calculation**

> EXAMPLE:
>
> - If Emily is thinking about buying each of the 11 guests at her party a fancy hat costing £4.95, she could estimate the cost by rounding the numbers to 10 and £5.
>
> - This would give an estimated cost of £50
>
> - The cost would really be £54.45 but the estimate is all Emily needs so that she knows roughly what the total cost would be.

Supermarket shopping

When you next go shopping at a supermarket, estimate the total cost of the items in your basket or trolley. See how close you are. Perhaps the person who is closest to the checkout total could win a prize!

You may be surprised to find that, with practice and suitable strategies, you can improve your estimation skills.

TOP TIP

Don't miss an opportunity to add value to a shopping trip!

Decorating

Estimate the cost of decorating your bedroom. For example, you might wish to cover the walls with wallpaper, in which case you would first need to find out roughly how many rolls of paper you would need. You could then check at the local DIY store to see what the cost of your chosen paper would be. You may wish to paint the walls, in which case you would need to take into consideration

- the area to be painted

- the number of coats of paint needed

- the area covered by one tin of paint

- the cost of the paint – perhaps comparing the cost of different sizes of tin!

We can estimate

- a **measurement**

EXAMPLE:

How might you estimate the length of this pencil?

- You could imagine how many identical pencils would fit end to end beside your ruler.

- If you think you could fit three pencils, then your estimate might be 10 cm but if you think you could fit in three and a bit pencils, or that three pencils would stretch too far, then you could adjust your estimate.

- Now, measure the length of the pencil, as accurately as possible, with your ruler.

- You will find that your measurement, to the nearest millimetre, is 9.7 cm, so an estimated length of 10 cm is realistic.

TOP TIP

When a tradesman is asked for an estimate, it is important for all concerned that the estimate is realistic!

- In the same way, we could estimate an area, a volume, a mass, an angle or any other measurement.

- It must be remembered that **all measurements are approximate**. When we measured the length of the pencil as 9.7 cm, it could really be 9.69 cm or 9.71 cm (or 9.70635742 cm, if we could measure to that degree of accuracy!)

How long is it?

Estimate the length of the fish in the drawing.

Now measure the length of the fish, as accurately as you can, and see how good your estimate was.

More measurements

Estimate the lengths of various items in your home or school and then check with a ruler or tape measure.

Estimating non-linear distances is rather more tricky! Try estimating the girth of a tree or the wrist measurement of a friend!

What is the area?

Without making any measurements, estimate the area of this rectangle and write down your estimate.

Now, measure the length and width of the rectangle and calculate the area.

Estimate the area of your hand and then check by drawing an outline of your hand on centimetre squared paper.

We can estimate

- a **position on a scale or number line**

EXAMPLE: On the number line below, the approximate position of 33 is indicated.

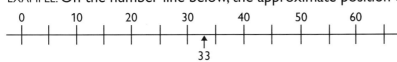

Walking home

Estimate how long it will take you to walk from home to the nearest bus stop or shop. Then time yourself and see how close you were.

Questions

The answers are at the back of the book.

1.27 (i) Estimate the position of 4 on this number line. Mark it with a cross on a copy of the line. (1)

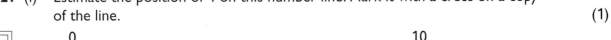

(ii) Estimate the position of 70 on this number line. Mark it with a cross on a copy of the line. (1)

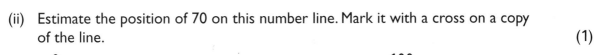

1.28 (i) Estimate (do not calculate exactly) the result of the multiplication 395×41 (1)

(ii) Estimate the result of the division $805 \div 9.8$ (1)

1.29 Alan has taken about an hour to read 31 pages of his mystery book. The book has 596 pages. About how many hours will it take Alan to read the whole book? (3)

Rounding integers

- It is very useful to be able to 'round' a whole number to give an **approximate** value.

- Sometimes it is helpful to **round up** and sometimes it is helpful to **round down**.

Study the following examples from everyday life.

EXAMPLE 1:

- If we are sharing 18 sweets between four children, they will receive four and a half sweets each.

- In this case, it is sensible to round down. Each child will receive four sweets and there will be two sweets left over.

EXAMPLE 2:

- If seven people are going to eat half a pizza each, then altogether they will eat three and a half pizzas.

- In this case it is sensible to round up. They will need to buy four pizzas.

- We can round numbers to the **nearest ten**, to the **nearest hundred**, to the **nearest fifty** and so on.

EXAMPLE 1: rounding 345 to the nearest ten.

- An abacus can help you to understand this.

- Draw, or imagine, a vertical line to the right of the tens column.

- Look at the column immediately to the right of the vertical line.

- If, in that column (the units column, in this case), there are beads above the horizontal line on the abacus, then we round up. We add one bead to the tens column and remove all the beads from the units column.

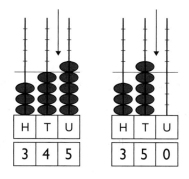

So 345 rounded to the nearest ten is 350

EXAMPLE 2: rounding 1549 to the nearest hundred.

- Draw, or imagine, a vertical line to the right of the hundreds column.

- Look at the column immediately to the right of the vertical line.

- If, in that column (the tens column, in this case), there were beads above the horizontal line, then we would round up, but there are not, so we round down.

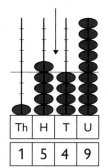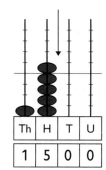

So 1549 rounded to the nearest hundred is 1500

The rules are:

- **Rounding up**: add 1 to the digit to the left of the vertical line and replace all digits to the right of the vertical line with zeros.

- **Rounding down**: simply replace all digits to the right of the vertical line with zeros.

EXAMPLE 1: rounding 3458 to the nearest ten.

3 4 5|8   round up   3 4 6 0

EXAMPLE 2: rounding 5498 to the nearest thousand.

5|4 9 8   round down   5 0 0 0

EXAMPLE 3: rounding 7852 to the nearest hundred.

7 8|5 2   round up   7 9 0 0

- If the number immediately to the right of the vertical line is a 5 or more, we round up.

- If the number immediately to the right of the vertical line is a 4 or less, we round down.

EXAMPLE 4: rounding to the nearest ten.

4 2 3	4	becomes	4 2 3 0
4 2 3	5	becomes	4 2 4 0
4 2 3	6	becomes	4 2 4 0
4 2 4	3	becomes	4 2 4 0
4 2 4	5	becomes	4 2 5 0

Rounding decimals to integers

The rules are very similar when rounding decimals to the nearest integer (whole number).

EXAMPLE 1: rounding 8.6 to the nearest integer gives 9

EXAMPLE 2: rounding 8.4 to the nearest integer gives 8

EXAMPLE 3: rounding 8.5 to the nearest integer gives 9

EXAMPLE 4: rounding 8.49 to the nearest integer gives 8

- Note that when rounding decimals to the nearest integer, we do not replace digits to the right of the point with zeros.

Rounding decimals to a number of decimal places

When we round a decimal to a number of decimal places, we follow the same basic rules.

EXAMPLE 1:

| 3.444 | is | 3.44 | written to 2 decimal places (2 d.p.) |
| | | 3.4 | written to 1 d.p. |

EXAMPLE 2:

| 7.245 | is | 7.25 | written to 2 d.p. |
| | | 7.2 | written to 1 d.p. |

EXAMPLE 3:

| 5.993 | is | 5.99 | written to 2 d.p. |
| | | 6.0 | written to 1 d.p. |

Rounding numbers to a number of significant figures

AIM HIGH

When rounding any number (integer or decimal) to a number of significant figures, again we follow the same basic rules.

EXAMPLE 1:

3594	is	3590	written to 3 significant figures (s.f.)
		3600	written to 2 s.f.
		4000	written to 1 s.f.

It is important to remember to put in zeros where required.

In the above example, the **0**s in 3590, 3600 and 4000 are not significant, but they are essential!

EXAMPLE 2:

39.57	is	39.6	written to 3 s.f.
		40	written to 2 s.f. (the zero is significant)
		40	written to 1 s.f. (the zero is not significant)

EXAMPLE 3:

97.09	is	97.1	written to 3 s.f.
		97	written to 2 s.f.
		100	written to 1 s.f. (the zeros are not significant)

Remember that **zeros on the right** are **sometimes** significant and sometimes not significant.

EXAMPLE 4:

Remember that **zeros on the left** are **never** significant.

| 0.6032 | is | 0.603 | to 3 s.f. |

Remember that **zeros 'in the middle'** are **always** significant.

| 0.6032 | is | 0.60 | to 2 s.f. |
| | | 0.6 | to 1 s.f. |

EXAMPLE 5:

304.03	is	304.0	to 4 s.f.
		304	to 3 s.f.
		300	to 2 s.f.
		300	to 1 s.f.

To do

Did you know?

Find some interesting statistics, such as the heights of mountains, or something to do with your hobby, and round the figures to the nearest ten, hundred etc, or to a number of significant figures.

Questions

The answers are at the back of the book.

1.30 (i) Write 485 to the nearest ten.   (1)

     (ii) Write 845 to the nearest hundred.   (1)

    (iii) Write 3.482 to the nearest whole number.   (1)

Multiple choice questions

In these questions you should write the letter of the correct answer.

1.31 How many of these have the answer 4000?   (1)

4060	written to the nearest hundred
3499	written to the nearest thousand
4005	written to the nearest ten
4005	written to the nearest hundred
4005	written to the nearest thousand
3500	written to 1 significant figure
4099	written to 2 significant figures

    A: 2   B: 3   C: 4   D: 5   E: 6

1.32 Which of the estimates below do you think is the best estimate for the number of one pound coins which could be placed, touching each other and the sheet, round the edge of a sheet of A4 paper?   (1)

    A: **40**   B: **50**   C: **60**   D: **70**   E: **80**

1.33 Which *one* of the following descriptions correctly describes 43.50?   (1)

    A: **43.512**   written to 3 significant figures

    B: **43.479**   written to 1 decimal place

    C: **43.509**   written to 4 significant figures

    D: **43.499**   written to 3 significant figures

    E: **43.499**   written to 2 decimal places

1.4 FRACTIONS, DECIMALS, PERCENTAGES AND RATIO

Proper fractions

In the fraction $\frac{2}{3}$ (two thirds) the bottom number (the **denominator**) tells us how many pieces a whole has been divided into, and the top number (the **numerator**) tells us how many of the pieces we have.

- In $\frac{2}{3}$ we have two of the three pieces.

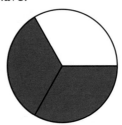

- In $\frac{2}{5}$ we have two of the five pieces.

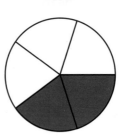

- We can write $\frac{2}{3} > \frac{2}{5}$ because $\frac{2}{3}$ is larger than $\frac{2}{5}$

Equivalent fractions

In these two diagrams (right) you will see that 3 pieces of a cake cut into 4 pieces is the same amount of cake as 6 pieces of a cake cut into 8 pieces.

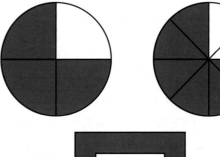

- $\frac{3}{4}$ and $\frac{6}{8}$ are **equivalent fractions**.

We can imagine a machine which makes equivalent fractions.

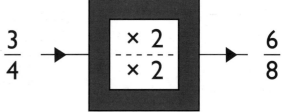

$$\frac{3}{4} \rightarrow \boxed{\begin{array}{c} \times 2 \\ \hline \times 2 \end{array}} \rightarrow \frac{6}{8}$$

- It simply multiplies the numerator and denominator by the same number.

EXAMPLE 1:

- $\frac{3}{4}$ can be changed into the equivalent fractions $\frac{6}{8}$ (machine set to ×2), $\frac{9}{12}$ (×3), $\frac{12}{16}$ (×4)

  and so on.

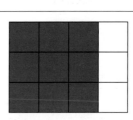

$$\frac{3}{4} = \frac{9}{12}$$

EXAMPLE 2:

- $\frac{2}{3}$ can be changed into the equivalent fractions $\frac{4}{6}$ (machine set to ×2), $\frac{6}{9}$ (×3), $\frac{8}{12}$ (×4) and so on.

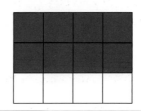

$$\frac{2}{3} = \frac{8}{12}$$

- In the examples above, both $\frac{3}{4}$ and $\frac{2}{3}$ can be changed into equivalent fractions with denominator 12
- This can be very useful when we are comparing fractions.

Writing a fraction in its simplest form (lowest terms)

If we consider the equivalent fraction machine put into reverse, by dividing both numerator and denominator by the same number, we can sometimes find **simpler equivalent fractions**.

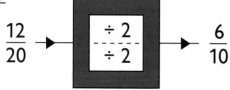

EXAMPLE 1:

- $\frac{12}{20}$ can be simplified to $\frac{6}{10}$ (by dividing both numerator and denominator by 2) and this is a simpler fraction.

- We can continue by dividing both numerator and denominator by 2 again to give $\frac{3}{5}$ which cannot be simplified further.

- We say that $\frac{3}{5}$ is the fraction in its **simplest form** (**lowest terms**).

EXAMPLE 2:

- $\frac{12}{15}$ in its simplest form is $\frac{4}{5}$ (divide numerator and denominator by 3)

For the rest of this section on fractions, we will represent one whole by the fraction strip on the right.

Comparing proper fractions

If we wish to **compare two fractions**, then we need to compare the **equivalent fractions** with the same denominator.

- We saw earlier that both $\frac{3}{4}$ and $\frac{2}{3}$ can be changed into equivalent fractions with denominator 12 and we say that, for these two fractions, 12 is a **common denominator**.

- The diagram shows fraction strips for $\frac{3}{4}$ $\left(\frac{9}{12}\right)$ and $\frac{2}{3}$ $\left(\frac{8}{12}\right)$

- It is clear that $\frac{3}{4}$ is the larger and the difference between them is $\frac{1}{12}$

Ordering proper fractions

We can put fractions in order of size by comparing them, as above.

Subtracting proper fractions

AIM HIGH

When subtracting with fractions it is necessary to change them to equivalent fractions with a common denominator first.

- In the diagram above, the difference between $\frac{3}{4}$ and $\frac{2}{3}$ is $\frac{1}{12}$

- We can write the subtraction calculation as
  $\frac{3}{4} - \frac{2}{3} = \frac{9}{12} - \frac{8}{12}$ (change to equivalent fractions with the same denominator) $= \frac{1}{12}$

- We can subtract proper fractions when they have the same denominator.

Adding proper fractions

EXAMPLE 1:

- The fraction strips (right) represent one whole, $\frac{1}{3}$ and $\frac{1}{2}$

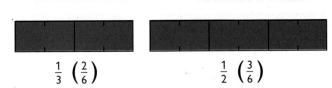

- To add $\frac{1}{3}$ and $\frac{1}{2}$ we need to consider the equivalent fractions with a common denominator.

$$\frac{1}{3}\left(\frac{2}{6}\right) \qquad \frac{1}{2}\left(\frac{3}{6}\right)$$

- In this case the lowest (smallest) common denominator is 6

- We can write the addition calculation as

$$\frac{1}{3} + \frac{1}{2}$$

$$= \frac{2}{6} + \frac{3}{6} \qquad \text{change to equivalent fractions with the same denominator}$$

$$= \frac{5}{6}$$

EXAMPLE 2:

- The fraction strips (right) represent $\frac{1}{3}, \frac{3}{4}$ and 1

$$\frac{1}{3}\left(\frac{4}{12}\right) \qquad \frac{3}{4}\left(\frac{9}{12}\right)$$

- In this case, the lowest common denominator (the lowest multiple of both 3 and 4) is 12 so we need to change both fractions to twelfths.

one whole

- We can write the calculation as

$$\frac{1}{3} + \frac{3}{4}$$

$$= \frac{4}{12} + \frac{9}{12}$$

$$= \frac{13}{12}$$

- The answer to Example 2, above, is interesting because $\frac{13}{12}$ is larger than one whole $\left(\frac{12}{12}\right)$.

- We say that $\frac{13}{12}$ is an **improper fraction**.

- Improper fractions are sometimes referred to as '**top heavy**' fractions.

Improper fractions and mixed numbers

In an **improper fraction**, the number of parts we have is more than one whole. In the previous case, we have thirteen twelfths.

- There are twelve twelfths in one whole so, in Example 2 on page 36, we have one whole and an extra twelfth. We can write this as $1\frac{1}{12}$

$1\frac{1}{12}$ is an example of a **mixed number**.

- A mixed number has a whole number part and a proper fraction part.

- Mixed numbers can be changed into improper fractions and vice versa.

EXAMPLE 1:

$1\frac{1}{2} \rightarrow \frac{2}{2} + \frac{1}{2} \rightarrow \frac{3}{2}$ One and a half is the same as three halves.

EXAMPLE 2:

$\frac{7}{4} \rightarrow \frac{4}{4} + \frac{3}{4} \rightarrow 1\frac{3}{4}$ Seven quarters is the same as one whole (four quarters), with three extra quarters.

AIM HIGH

When we add or subtract with mixed numbers, we may need to change the mixed numbers into improper fractions first.

EXAMPLE: $1\frac{1}{2} - \frac{3}{4}$

$= \frac{3}{2} - \frac{3}{4}$ mixed number changed to improper fraction

$= \frac{6}{4} - \frac{3}{4}$ $\frac{3}{2}$ changed to equivalent fraction with denominator 4

$= \frac{3}{4}$ 6 quarters minus 3 quarters gives 3 quarters

To do

Card game

This is a game for two players. You will need a set of cards numbered 1 to 9

| 1 | 2 | 3 | 4 | 5 | 6 | 7 | 8 | 9 |

Shuffle the cards and give each player four cards, leaving the remaining cards hidden.
Take it in turns to make up your own challenges, such as:

- who can make the largest proper fraction

- who can make the smallest improper fraction

- who can make a fraction that can be simplified.

$$\frac{3}{5} < \frac{7}{9}$$

When you have run out of ideas for challenges, shuffle the cards and deal them out again.

Multiplying with fractions

Remember that 'of' means multiply, so 'half of one third' means
$$\frac{1}{2} \times \frac{1}{3}$$

- In the diagram below, you will see a whole, a third and half of a third.

 one whole

 one third $\frac{1}{3}$ half of one third $\frac{1}{6}$

- Half of a third is clearly $\frac{1}{6}$

- We can write the calculation $\frac{1}{2} \times \frac{1}{3}$

$$= \frac{1}{6}$$

Multiplying the two numerators gives the numerator of the result: $1 \times 1 = 1$

Multiplying the two denominators gives the denominator of the result: $2 \times 3 = 6$

- The same method works for the multiplication of all proper fractions.

EXAMPLE 1:

$\frac{1}{4} \times \frac{1}{5} = \frac{1}{20}$ (a quarter of a fifth)

EXAMPLE 2:

$\frac{2}{3} \times \frac{1}{4} = \frac{2}{12}$ (two thirds of a quarter, or a quarter of two thirds)

We can simplify this result to $\frac{1}{6}$

EXAMPLE 3:

$\frac{2}{3} \times \frac{3}{5} = \frac{6}{15} = \frac{2}{5}$ in its simplest form (lowest terms)

Dividing with fractions

EXAMPLE 1:

- Suppose that you have half a bar of chocolate and want to share it between three people.

- You have $\frac{1}{2} \div 3$

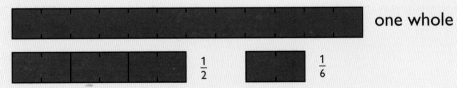 one whole

$\frac{1}{2}$ $\frac{1}{6}$

- Each person will receive $\frac{1}{6}$ of the bar of chocolate.

EXAMPLE 2:

- Suppose that you now have two bars of chocolate and want to see how many people could be given one third each.

- You have $2 \div \frac{1}{3}$

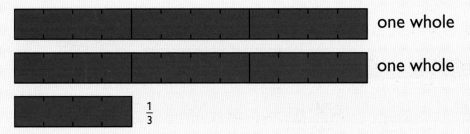

one whole

one whole

$\frac{1}{3}$

- Looking at the diagrams you can see that six people could be given a third of a bar of chocolate each.

EXAMPLE 3:

- Imagine you have half a bar of chocolate and want to see how many people can receive a quarter each.

- You have $\frac{1}{2} \div \frac{1}{4}$

$\frac{1}{2}$

$\frac{1}{4}$

- Looking at the diagrams you can see that there are two quarters in a half, so the result of $\frac{1}{2} \div \frac{1}{4}$ must be 2

In the examples above, the diagrams help you to understand what happens.

The usual method for dividing with fractions can appear to be magic! Let us see how this works with the last example $\frac{1}{2} \div \frac{1}{4}$

- We can write $\frac{1}{2} \div \frac{1}{4} \rightarrow \frac{1}{2} \times \frac{4}{1} \rightarrow \frac{4}{2} \rightarrow 2$

- We have changed the division sign to a multiplication sign and 'turned the second fraction, $\frac{1}{4}$, upside down' as $\frac{4}{1}$ (we have written its **reciprocal**).

EXAMPLE 4:

- $\frac{3}{4} \div \frac{1}{2} \rightarrow \frac{3}{4} \times \frac{2}{1} \rightarrow \frac{6}{4} \rightarrow \frac{3}{2} \rightarrow 1\frac{1}{2}$

EXAMPLE 5:

- $\frac{1}{2} \div \frac{3}{4} \rightarrow \frac{1}{2} \times \frac{4}{3} \rightarrow \frac{4}{6} \rightarrow \frac{2}{3}$

Fraction strips

Use a strip of 24 squares as the whole, as shown below on the left.

Make several copies of the strip and then from these make and label your own fraction strips.

$\frac{1}{24}$

$\frac{1}{2}$ (12 squares)

$\frac{1}{3}$ (8 squares)

$\frac{1}{6}$ (4 squares)

$\frac{1}{12}$

$\frac{1}{4}$ (6 squares)

$\frac{1}{8}$

(9 squares)

$\frac{3}{8}$

one whole (24 squares)

$\frac{1}{4}$ (6 squares)

$\frac{1}{3}$ (8 squares)

$\frac{1}{2}$ will be a strip of 12 squares $\frac{1}{12}$ will be a strip of 2 squares

$\frac{1}{3}$ will be a strip of 8 squares $\frac{1}{4}$ will be a strip of 6 squares

$\frac{1}{6}$ will be a strip of 4 squares $\frac{1}{8}$ will be a strip of 3 squares

In addition to those listed above, make others such as $\frac{2}{3}, \frac{3}{4}, \frac{5}{8}, \frac{7}{12}$ and so on.

Placing your fraction strips alongside the 'whole' strip of 24 squares, see how many different ways you can make up the whole, as in Example 1 on the left.

EXAMPLE 1:

Questions

The answers are at the back of the book.

1.34 In this strip of squares, five out of the nine have been shaded to show the fraction $\frac{5}{9}$

Sketch a similar diagram to show the fraction $\frac{5}{7}$ (2)

1.35 Find $\frac{2}{3}$ of 54 kilograms. (2)

1.36 Sandra's pencil was 147 mm long at the beginning of term. At the end of term the pencil was $\frac{4}{7}$ its original length. How long was Sandra's pencil at the end of term? (2)

1.37 (i) Which is bigger, $\frac{1}{11}$ or $\frac{1}{12}$? (1)

(ii) Which is bigger, $\frac{3}{5}$ or $\frac{7}{10}$? (1)

1.38 (i) Shanna has drawn a machine which finds equivalent fractions.

Here the machine is shown changing $\frac{3}{4}$ to eighths.

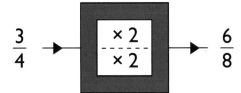

On a copy of the diagram below, fill in the details to show how the machine can change $\frac{2}{3}$ to twelfths. (2)

equivalent fraction machine

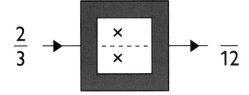

(ii) Shanna has now put the machine into reverse so that it can find the simplest form of a fraction.

On a copy of the diagram below, fill in the details to show how the machine can find the simplest form of the fraction $\frac{12}{21}$ (2)

simplest form machine

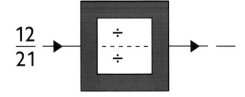

Fractions and decimals

- To change a fraction to a **decimal**, we change it to an equivalent fraction with a denominator (bottom number) of 10 or 100 or 1000

- We can then write the numerator of the fraction with the correct place values.

EXAMPLE 1:

$\frac{1}{2}$ is the same as $\frac{5}{10}$ (5 tenths)

U. t
0 . 5

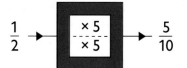

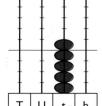

EXAMPLE 2:

$\frac{3}{5}$ is the same as $\frac{6}{10}$

U. t
0 . 6

T	U	t	h
	0 • 5		

EXAMPLE 3:

$\frac{3}{4}$ is the same as $\frac{75}{100}$

U.th
0 .75

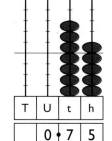

T	U	t	h
	0 • 7	5	

- We could get the same result by dividing the numerator by the denominator.

EXAMPLE 4:

$$2 \overline{)1.0} \qquad 4 \overline{)3.00} \qquad 8 \overline{)5.000}$$
$$0.5 \qquad 0.75 \qquad 0.625$$

- Some fractions cannot be changed into a fraction with a denominator of 10, 100, 1000 or any multiple of 10 so for these fractions we must divide the numerator by the denominator.

EXAMPLE 5:

$\frac{1}{3}$ cannot be changed to an equivalent fraction with denominator 10, 100, 1000 or any multiple of 10, so we divide 1 by 3

$$3 \overline{)1.000\ 000\ 000\ \ldots}$$
$$0.333\ 333\ 333\ \ldots$$

$\frac{1}{3} \rightarrow 0.333\ 333\ 333\ 333\ \ldots$

AIM HIGH

This is an example of a **recurring decimal** and we can write this in shorthand as 0.$\dot{3}$ where the little dot over the 3 indicates that the 3 recurs.

It is interesting to see what happens with other fractions.

EXAMPLE 6:

$$7 \overline{)1.000\ 000\ 000\ 000 \ldots}$$
$$0.142\ 857\ 142\ 857 \ldots$$

We can write this recurring decimal as 0.$\overline{142\ 857}$ where the line over the figures shows the repeating unit.

Decimals and percentages

A **percentage** is a number of parts out of 100

- You have probably seen a 'percentage complete' bar on the screen when a computer is downloading files or making updates.

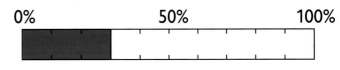

0% 50% 100%

- To change a decimal to a percentage, we simply multiply by 100

| EXAMPLE 1: 0.5 gives 50% | EXAMPLE 2: 0.6 gives 60% | EXAMPLE 3: 0.75 gives 75% |

- $\frac{1}{3}$ may be written as 0.33 recurring ($0.\dot{3}$) or $33\frac{1}{3}$%

Game of Triminoes

A **trimino** looks like this.

It has a proper fraction, a decimal and a percentage.

The game is played rather like dominoes where a player has to match up the fractions, decimals and percentages which are equivalent.

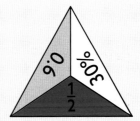

A sample set of triminoes is available as a downloadable worksheet, but it is much more fun if you make up your own!

The diagram (right) shows a game of triminoes in action. You may be able to place a piece in a position where it makes two matches!

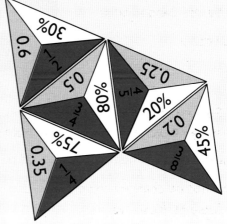

Questions

The answers are at the back of the book.

1.39 Freddie's grandfather gave him £25 and he decided to save 80% of it. How much did Freddie save? (2)

1.40 Copy and complete the table below, showing equivalent fractions, decimals and percentages.

Fraction (in simplest form)	$\frac{2}{5}$			$\frac{7}{10}$
Decimal		0.25	0.8	
Percentage	40%	35%		

(9)

Ratio

Fractions (such as $\frac{3}{4}$) compare the number of parts we have (in this case 3) to the total number of parts in the whole (in this case 4).

   $\frac{3}{4}$ of this square is shaded.

Ratios can do the same thing, but they can also be much more useful.

- Looking at the diagram above, the ratio of the area of the shaded part of the square to the area of the whole square can be written as 3 : 4

- This corresponds to the fraction $\frac{3}{4}$

- We can compare the area of the shaded part to the area of the unshaded part as the ratio 3 : 1

- If we wish to compare the area of the unshaded part to the area of the shaded part, then the ratio is 1 : 3

- With a ratio, we can compare more than two things. We could write the ratio area of square : area of shaded part : area of unshaded part as 4 : 3 : 1

Look at this group of shapes.

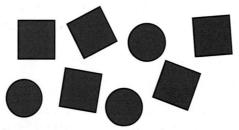

- There are five squares and three circles.

- The fraction of the shapes which are square is $\frac{5}{8}$

- The ratio of the number of squares to the total number of shapes is 5 : 8 but with ratio, we can go further.

- The ratio of the number of squares to the number of circles is 5 : 3

Some fractions can be simplified.

- For example $\frac{6}{8}$ can be simplified to $\frac{3}{4}$

- Some ratios can be simplified in the same way, so 10 : 6 simplifies to 5 : 3

Proportion

A '**proportion of something**' is a way of describing a part of the whole.

- This can be expressed as a fraction or a percentage.

EXAMPLE 1:

- In a school of 300 students, there are 201 boys; the proportion of boys in the class is about two-thirds.

EXAMPLE 2:

- Air is made up mostly of the gases nitrogen (78.09%) and oxygen (20.95%) with a little argon (0.93%), carbon dioxide (0.03%), water vapour and rare gases; the proportion of nitrogen in the air is about 78%

EXAMPLE 3:

- The proportion of the population that is left-handed is about one in every eight.

EXAMPLE 4:

- A blackcurrant drink should be diluted with water – the recommendation is 1 part blackcurrant concentrate with 4 parts of water.

EXAMPLE 5:

- If you have a recipe to make 12 buns, but you wish to make more than 12, then you will need to increase the quantities of the ingredients **in proportion**.

Proportions

Start with a large lump of modelling clay or a ball of 'sticky tack'. Try to split this into two pieces with equal mass, then into three pieces with equal mass, then four pieces…

You may be surprised at how good you can become at estimating a proportion of something.

Now, we don't often need to do this with sticky tack, but this is a very useful idea in everyday life.

EXAMPLE:

A pack of butter bought at a shop will probably have a mass of 250 g. A recipe for shortbread may say that you should add 150 g of butter. You should be able to estimate roughly where to position the knife to cut off the right amount of butter.

Proportion

We sometimes hear the words:

- 'proportional representation'
- 'a proportional response by the police'
- 'out of all proportion'.

Find out what these mean.

Fractions of numbers

To find a unit fraction of a number, we can

- divide the number by the denominator of the fraction, or

- multiply the number by the fraction.

EXAMPLE 1: half of 72	EXAMPLE 2: a fifth of 45
We can say	We can say
• $72 \div 2 = 36$, or	• $45 \div 5 = 9$, or
• $72 \times \frac{1}{2} = 36$	• $45 \times \frac{1}{5} = 9$

To find a non-unit fraction of a number, we simply multiply by the fraction.

> EXAMPLE 3: $\frac{3}{4}$ of 60
>
> - $60 \times \frac{3}{4} = 45$
>
> - We divide by the denominator (in this case 4) to find $\frac{1}{4}$ of 60 and then multiply by the numerator (in this case 3) to find $\frac{3}{4}$ of 60
>
> EXAMPLE 4: $\frac{4}{5}$ of 80
>
> - $80 \times \frac{4}{5} = 64$
>
> - We divide by the denominator (in this case 5) to find $\frac{1}{5}$ of 80 and then multiply by the numerator (in this case 4) to find $\frac{4}{5}$ of 80

Fractional parts of quantities

To find a fractional part of a quantity, we follow the same procedure as with fractions of numbers.

EXAMPLE 1: a quarter of 70 cl	EXAMPLE 2: $\frac{2}{3}$ of 6 kg
• $70 \times \frac{1}{4} = 17.5$ so we have 17.5 cl	• $6 \times \frac{2}{3} = 4$ so we have 4 kg

Percentage parts of quantities

AIM
HIGH

When we want to find a percentage part of a quantity, we can use common sense (as for 10% or 50%) or we can multiply by an equivalent fraction or decimal.

EXAMPLE 1: 10% of 70 kg	EXAMPLE 2: 50% of 3 litres
We can do	We can do
• $70 \div 10 = 7$ or	• $3 \div 2 = 1.5$ or
• $70 \times \frac{1}{10} = 7$ or	• $3 \times \frac{1}{2} = 1.5$ or
• $70 \times 0.1 = 7$ so we have 7 kg	• $3 \times \frac{5}{10} = 1.5$ or
	• $3 \times 0.5 = 1.5$ so we have 1.5 litres

For other percentage parts of quantities it is sometimes easier to find 10% or 50% first and then work in a step-by-step method.

EXAMPLE 3:	30% of £4.50	
We can do	• 10% of £4.50 is 45 pence	(dividing £4.50 by 10)
	• 30% of £4.50 is 3 × 45 pence which is £1.35	
EXAMPLE 4:	55% of 3 tonnes	
We can do	• 50% of 3 tonnes is 1.5 tonnes	
	• 5% of 3 tonnes is 0.15 tonnes	(dividing 50% by 10)
	• 55% of 3 tonnes is 1.65 tonnes	(adding 50% and 5%)

Questions

The answers are at the back of the book.

1.41 Jo has three rabbits and seven hamsters.

    (i)   What is the ratio of the number of hamsters to the number of rabbits? Answer in the form _ : _   (2)

    (ii) What is the ratio of the number of hamsters to the total number of pets?   (2)

1.42 *Yummy* sweets are sold in two sizes of packets – small and large. Each packet contains chocolates and mints in the ratio 5 : 4

    (i)   In a small packet there are 10 chocolates.

        (a) How many mints are there in a small packet?   (1)

        (b) What is the total number of sweets in a small packet?   (1)

    (ii) A large packet contains 36 sweets altogether. How many of each type of sweet are there?   (2)

1.43 Amy, Barbara and Clarissa share a box of 300 stamps in the ratio 4 : 5 : 6

How many stamps will each girl receive?   (3)

Multiple choice questions

In these questions you should write the letter of the correct answer.

1.44 How many of the following are larger than $\frac{1}{2}$?   (1)

$\frac{2}{5}$ $\frac{11}{20}$ **0.49** $\frac{51}{99}$ $\frac{3}{7}$ **5%** $\frac{15}{31}$ **55%** $\frac{7}{15}$

    A: 3   B: 4   C: 5   D: 6   E: 7

1.45 Which one of the following fractions is **not** equivalent to $\frac{2}{3}$?   (1)

    A: $\frac{24}{36}$ B: $\frac{16}{24}$ C: $\frac{18}{27}$ D: $\frac{32}{52}$ E: $\frac{90}{135}$

1.46 Which is the largest of these fractions?   (1)

    A: $\frac{2}{3}$ B: $\frac{3}{4}$ C: $\frac{4}{5}$ D: $\frac{5}{6}$ E: $\frac{6}{7}$

2 CALCULATIONS

Can you imagine a world without calculations? Calculations are everywhere – working out how many days it is to your birthday, working out how much change you can expect from a shopkeeper, finding the cost of three ice lollies, calculating how much each four people will receive if they share a £10 prize.

2.1 NUMBER OPERATIONS

The four basic operations

In Chapter 1 the diagrams representing the four operations showed **number strips**.

A simple **number line** could be used instead. Here are a few quick reminders, using number lines this time.

Addition

- 7 + 11 = 18

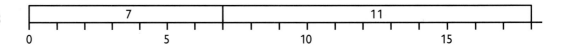

Subtraction

- 13 – 9 = 4

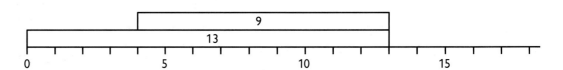

Multiplication

- 6 × 3 = 18

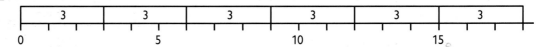

Division – exact

- 16 ÷ 4 = 4

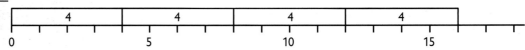

Division – with a remainder

- 16 ÷ 3 = 5 remainder 1

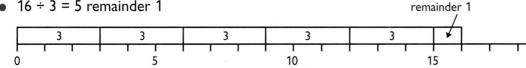

Number facts

Addition and subtraction facts

- Addition and subtraction facts come in groups of four.

EXAMPLE 1:		EXAMPLE 2:	
3 + 7 = 10	10 – 7 = 3	237 + 113 = 350	350 – 237 = 113
7 + 3 = 10	10 – 3 = 7	113 + 237 = 350	350 – 113 = 237

TOP TIP

Practice may not make perfect, but it certainly helps!

- When carrying out an addition or subtraction, it may sometimes help to work with one of the other three facts.

EXAMPLE 3: $72 - 18 = 54$ It may be easier to think of this as 'something $+ 18$ gives 72'
$? + 18 = 72$

Multiplication and division facts

- Multiplication and division facts also come in groups of four.

EXAMPLE 1:		EXAMPLE 2:	
$3 \times 7 = 21$	$21 \div 7 = 3$	$37 \times 3 = 111$	$111 \div 37 = 3$
$7 \times 3 = 21$	$21 \div 3 = 7$	$3 \times 37 = 111$	$111 \div 3 = 37$

- When carrying out a multiplication or division, it may sometimes help to work with one of the other three facts.

EXAMPLE 3: $72 \div 18 = 4$ It may be easier to think of this as 'something $\times 18$ gives 72'
$? \times 18 = 72$

The multiplication table

We looked at the multiplication table in Chapter 1 (page 10). You will remember that

- the table is symmetrical about the shaded diagonal which consists of the square numbers – so if you know $7 \times 6 = 42$, you also know $6 \times 7 = 42$

- there are relatively few multiplication facts which some people find difficult to remember – the six indicated by darker shading – and it should not take long to learn those six

- the table may also be used to help with division – both exact and with a remainder.

1	2	3	4	5	6	7	8	9	10	11	12
2	4	6	8	10	12	14	16	18	20	22	24
3	6	9	12	15	18	21	24	27	30	33	36
4	8	12	16	20	24	28	32	36	40	44	48
5	10	15	20	25	30	35	40	45	50	55	60
6	12	18	24	30	36	42	48	54	60	66	72
7	14	21	28	35	42	49	56	63	70	77	84
8	16	24	32	40	48	56	64	72	80	88	96
9	18	27	36	45	54	63	72	81	90	99	108
10	20	30	40	50	60	70	80	90	100	110	120
11	22	33	44	55	66	77	88	99	110	121	132
12	24	36	48	60	72	84	96	108	120	132	144

EXAMPLE 1:
For 63 divided by 9 we
• look along the 9 times row until we reach 63
• look up the column to find that 9×7 is 63, so 63 divided by 9 is 7
In this case, the division is exact.
EXAMPLE 2:
For 50 divided by 8 we
• look along the 8 times row until we reach 50 or a number which is close to 50
• notice that 50 is not there
• notice that 48 (8×6) and 56 (8×7) are there
• realise that 8 will not 'go into' 50 seven times exactly
• decide that 8 will go into 50 six times, with **remainder** 2 ($50 - 48$).

To do

Personal best

Make a copy of the 7 × 7 square grid below.

×	7	5	9	4	6	8	3
7							
8							
3							
5							
9							
4							
6							

TOP TIP

It might be a good idea to repeat this personal challenge on a regular basis – perhaps once a week.

- Complete the multiplication table and make a note of your time.

After a few minutes' break, make another copy of the grid but vary the positions of the numerals 3 to 9 along the top and down the side.

- Time yourself again and make a note of your time.

- Is it possible to improve your personal best time with practice?

- Do you perform better early in the morning or later in the day?

You might like to organise a competition with your friends. To be fair, everyone should have an identical grid at the start and you will probably need a time-keeper!

Useful strategies for finding multiplication facts

Using doubling and halving

For

- 3×   double and then add the number

EXAMPLE:	3 × 7	we get 14 and then 21 (14 + 7)

- 4×   double and then double again

EXAMPLE:	4 × 7	we get 14, then 28

- 5×   multiply by 10 and then divide by 2

EXAMPLE:	5 × 7	we get 70, then 35

- 6×   do 5× as above and then add the number

EXAMPLE:	6 × 7	we get 70, then 35, then 42 (35 + 7)

  or, we could double, then double again, and add the first doubling result

EXAMPLE:	6 × 7	we get 14, then 28, then 42 (28 + 14)

- **7×** double, then double again, then double again, then subtract the number

  > EXAMPLE: 7 × 7   we get 14, then 28, then 56, then 49 (56 − 7)

- **8×** double, then double again, then double again

  > EXAMPLE: 8 × 7   we get 14, then 28, then 56

- **9×** multiply by 10 and then subtract the number

  > EXAMPLE: 9 × 7   we get 70, then 63 (70 − 7)

- **11×** multiply by 10 and then add the number

  > EXAMPLE: 11 × 7   we get 70, then 77 (70 + 7)

- **12×** multiply by 10 and then add double the number

  > EXAMPLE: 12 × 7   we get 70, then 84 (70 + 14)

Partitioning

When multiplying by larger numbers, we can make use of a similar idea, known as **partitioning**.

> EXAMPLE: 13 × 7   we get (10 × 7) + (3 × 7) which is 70 + 21, giving the result 91

Questions

The answers are at the back of the book.

Make five copies of this number line.

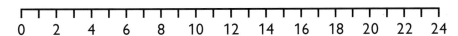

2.1 On the first copy of the number line, show the addition fact 7 + 13 = ?   (1)

2.2 On a different copy, show the subtraction fact 17 − 8 = ?   (1)

2.3 On a different copy, show the multiplication fact 5 × 3 = ?   (1)

2.4 On a different copy, show the division fact 21 ÷ 7 = ?   (1)

2.5 On a different copy, show what happens when we divide 23 by 6   (1)

2.6 Here is an addition fact:

17 + 24 = 41

Using the same numbers 17, 24 and 41 in each fact, write down three related addition/subtraction facts.   (3)

2.7 Here is a multiplication fact:

13 × 7 = 91

Using the same numbers 13, 7 and 91 in each fact, write down three related multiplication/division facts.   (3)

The order of operations

When there are several operations in a calculation, the order in which you do them can be very important.

AIM HIGH

Brackets can be used to show that the calculation inside them should be done first.

EXAMPLE 1:

$3 \times (4 + 3)$ here the brackets show that the addition should be done first
so we get 3×7 giving the answer 21

$3 \times 4 + 3$ without the brackets, we do the multiplication first
so we get $12 + 3$ giving the answer 15

EXAMPLE 2:

$4 \times 8 - 2 \times 3$ without the brackets we do the multiplications first and get
$32 - 6$ giving the answer 26

$4 \times (8 - 2 \times 3)$ here we do the calculations in the brackets first, so we get
$4 \times (8 - 6) \rightarrow 4 \times 2 \rightarrow 8$

Indices should be tackled next.

EXAMPLE 3:

Evaluate $3^2 \times 4$ we square 3 before we multiply by 4, so we get $9 \times 4 \rightarrow 36$

EXAMPLE 4:

Evaluate $3^2 - 2^3$ we deal with the indices first, so we get $9 - 8 \rightarrow 1$

Division and **multiplication** should be done next.

Addition and **subtraction** are tackled last.

EXAMPLE 5:

You are unlikely to meet a calculation as complicated as this one, but it shows the order in which the calculations should be completed.

Evaluate $5^2 + 6 \times (5 - 2) \div 3 - 2^3$

$\rightarrow$ $5^2 + 6 \times 3 \div 3 - 2^3$ **b**rackets dealt with

$\rightarrow$ $25 + 6 \times 3 \div 3 - 8$ **i**ndices dealt with

$\rightarrow$ $25 + 6 - 8$ **d**ivision and **m**ultiplication dealt with

$\rightarrow$ 23 **a**ddition and **s**ubtraction dealt with

AIM HIGH

The mnemonic **bidmas** may be useful in remembering the order of operations.

Some people may prefer a slightly different mnemonic **bodmas** where the letter **o** stands for 'of'.

Final score

Make a set of number cards with the numbers 2 to 9

| **2** | **3** | **4** | **5** | **6** | **7** | **8** | **9** |

Shuffle the cards and then select three cards at random.

Study the numbers carefully.

The idea is to combine any two of the numbers by addition, subtraction or multiplication and then divide by the third number, to give an integer (whole number) result.

EXAMPLE 1:

| **4** | **8** | **5** |

In this case, we can say 8 × 5 = 40 and then 40 ÷ 4 = 10, so the score is 10

EXAMPLE 2:

| **3** | **9** | **6** |

In this case there are several possibilities. We could say 3 + 9 = 12 and then 12 ÷ 6 = 2, so the score would be 2, or we could say 6 + 9 = 15 and then 15 ÷ 3 = 5, so the score would be 5, or we could say 6 × 9 = 54 and then 54 ÷ 3 = 18 so the score could be as high as 18

Is there any combination of cards which cannot give a whole number score?

You could make up your own rule, such as losing 10 points or missing a turn, if this happens.

Play the game with your friends.

Multiple choice questions

In these questions you should write the letter of the correct answer.

2.8   How many of these addition and subtraction facts have a result which is between
        40 and 50?   (1)

13 + 38	27 + 12	67 − 23	9 + 32	87 − 39
23 + 19	72 − 35	24 + 15	123 − 86	382 − 338
A: 3	B: 4	C: 5	D: 6	E: 7

2.9   Which of these multiplication and division facts has the largest result?   (1)

   A: **6 × 9**   B: **7 × 8**   C: **110 ÷ 2**   D: **280 ÷ 5**   E: **29 × 2**

2.2 MENTAL STRATEGIES

AIM HIGH

When tackling questions without paper and pencil or a calculator, a number of very useful strategies can be used.

Taking easier steps

- These examples make use of rounding to a convenient integer and then adjusting the result.

EXAMPLE 1:	3 × 99	do	3 × 100 − 3	→	300 − 3	→	297
EXAMPLE 2:	17 × 101	do	17 × 100 + 17	→	1700 + 17	→	1717
EXAMPLE 3:	9 × £5.99	do	9 × £6 − 9 pence	→	£54 − 9p	→	£53.91

- We can also use partitioning.

EXAMPLE 4:	58 × 7	do	(50 × 7) + (8 × 7)	→	350 + 56	→	406
EXAMPLE 5:	5.4 × 8	do	(5 × 8) + (0.4 × 8)	→	40 + 3.2	→	43.2

Doubling or halving

- It is often easier to double or halve several times than to do a more complicated calculation.

EXAMPLE 1:	£2.55 × 8	→	£5.10 × 4	→	£10.20 × 2	→ £20.40
EXAMPLE 2:	£30.60 ÷ 4	→	£15.30 ÷ 2	→	£7.65	

- We can also make use of 'near doubles' when multiplying by 7 or 9 (see page xx).

Multiplying or dividing by 5

- We make use of the fact that 5 is half of 10

EXAMPLE 1:	37 × 5	→	37 × 10 ÷ 2	→	370 ÷ 2	→	185
EXAMPLE 2:	425 ÷ 5	→	425 × 2 ÷ 10	→	850 ÷ 10	→	85

Help with adding and subtracting

- Study these examples and see why the strategy works.

EXAMPLE 1:	123 − 19	→	124 − 20	→	104

- Here we have increased both numbers by 1

EXAMPLE 2:	57 + 29	→	56 + 30	→	86

- Here we have increased one number by 1 and decreased the other number by 1

Making use of factors in division

- We can write an integer as the product of factors (not necessarily prime factors).

EXAMPLE 1: $108 \div 18$ → $54 \div 9$ → $18 \div 3$ →   6

- Because $18 = 2 \times 3 \times 3$ (or 2×9), we have divided by 2, then 3 and then 3 again (or we could have divided by 2 and then by 9).

EXAMPLE 2: $165 \div 15$ → $55 \div 5$ →   11

- Because $15 = 3 \times 5$, we have divided by 3 and then by 5

Making use of known facts

EXAMPLE 1: For the multiplication 0.8×3, we know that $8 \times 3 = 24$, so 0.8×3 must be 2.4

EXAMPLE 2: For the division $1.44 \div 1.2$, we know that $144 \div 12 = 12$, so $1.44 \div 1.2 = 1.2$

Using a step-by-step approach

- This is particularly useful when we are finding a fraction or percentage of something.

EXAMPLE 1: For $\frac{3}{8}$ of £24, first find $\frac{1}{8}$ of £24 (£3) and then multiply by 3 (£9)

EXAMPLE 2: For 15% of 12 kg, first find 10% of 12 kg (1.2 kg) and then find 5% of 12 kg (0.6 kg) and then add (1.8 kg)

Grouping numbers when adding

EXAMPLE 1: $37 + 49 + 23 + 31$ → $(37 + 23) + (49 + 31)$ → $60 + 80$ etc

EXAMPLE 2:   £4.50 + £1.75 + £9.25 + £5.50

Here we can think (£4.50 + £5.50) + (£1.75 + £9.25)   →   £10 + £11   etc

Making use of approximations

- It is always a good idea to know roughly what the answer should be. Common sense plays a large part in this.

EXAMPLE 1: 2.9×7 will be about 20 (a little less than 3×7 which is 21)

EXAMPLE 2: $41 + 197$ will be about 240

Going shopping

Next time your family go shopping in a supermarket, by grouping and approximating, see who can get closest to the total amount at the checkout.

Checking, using known facts

- We can make use of odd/even facts (see page 6) and we can check the units digits.

EXAMPLE 1:

The answer to the calculation 423 + 98 must

- be odd (because an odd number plus an even number always gives an odd number)
- end in 1 (since 3 + 8 = 11)

EXAMPLE 2:

The answer to the calculation 423 × 98 must

- be even (because an odd number times an even number always gives an even number)
- end in 4 (since 3 × 8 = 24)

Mental maths

Make up a mental test of ten questions where each question makes use of one, or more, of the ten strategies listed on pages 54–56. Try to involve all ten strategies somewhere.

Questions

For all questions in this section you should do no written working but simply write the answers. Do all the calculations in your head. Check that each answer is sensible.

2.10 Write the answers to the following multiplications:

    (i)   3 × 29   (1)

    (ii) 4 × 51   (1)

    (iii) 5 × 99   (1)

2.11 Write the answers to the following divisions:

    (i)   432 ÷ 12   (1)

    (ii) 184 ÷ 8   (1)

2.12 A farmer had 308 chickens in a pen.

    One day 41 chickens escaped.

    How many chickens remained in the pen?   (1)

2.13 There were 44 people on a coach.

    When the coach reached Glasgow, 29 people got off and 21 got on.

    How many people were now on the coach?   (1)

2.14 What is the cost of 19 fruit bars, costing 52 pence each?   (1)

2.15 Sally left home at 07:55 and cycled for 45 minutes to reach her school.
At what time did she arrive at school?   (1)

2.16 What is the smallest number, greater than 70, which divides exactly by 3?   (1)

2.17 A known division fact is 48 ÷ 3 = 16

Use this fact to help you to find the answers to the following:

(i)   480 ÷ 3   (1)

(ii) 48 ÷ 30   (1)

(iii) 4.8 ÷ 3   (1)

(iv) 4.8 ÷ 6   (1)

Multiple choice questions

In these questions you should write the letter of the correct answer.

2.18 Which of these calculations has the largest result?   (1)

A: **480 ÷ 60**   B: **4 × 1.5**   C: **45 − 36**   D: **4.5 + 3.5**   E: **15% of 40**

2.19 How many of these calculations have an odd number answer?   (1)

3 × 9	**24 ÷ 3**	**43 − 29**	**31 + 37**	**3²**	**245 ÷ 5**
100 − 47	**63 × 111**	**4³**	**120 − 17**	**8 + 7**	**18 × 9**
A: 5	B: 6	C: 7	D: 8	E: 9	

2.3 WRITTEN METHODS

These five important 'rules' may help you to avoid errors and gain more marks:

1. Make a mental estimate of the answer so that you know roughly what to expect.
2. Set out your calculations clearly and neatly.
3. Watch place value.
4. Check to make sure that your answer is sensible.
5. Don't forget to write the correct units, if appropriate.

Addition

EXAMPLE 1:

308 + 1975

```
      3 0 8
  + 1 9 7 5
    2 2 8 3
      1   1
```

When adding integers, remember to line up the units digits in the *right-hand column*.

The little 'carrying' digits are helpful.

EXAMPLE 2:

4.9 + 10.56

```
    T U . t  h
      4 . 9
  + 1 0 . 5  6
    1 5 . 4  6
          1
```

Writing the column headings may be helpful.

When adding decimals, remember that the units digits must be in the same column.

Notice the little 'carrying' digit.

EXAMPLE 3:

105.37 + 17.4 + 209.06

```
    1 0 5 . 3 7
      1 7 . 4
  + 2 0 9 . 0 6
    3 3 1 . 8 3
        2   1
```

Subtraction

EXAMPLE 1:

269 − 125

```
    H T U
    2 6 9
  - 1 2 5
    1 4 4
```

We take 5 units from 9 units, then we take 2 tens from 6 tens and finally we take 1 hundred from 2 hundreds.

EXAMPLE 2:

284 − 139

```
    2 8 4
  - 1 3 9
    1 4 5
```

We can't take 9 units from 4 units so it is necessary to change one of the tens into 10 units.

Then we have 14 − 9 units and 7 − 3 tens.

EXAMPLE 3:

300 − 143

```
    3 0 0
  − 1 4 3
    1 5 7
```

Here we can change one of the hundreds into 9 tens and 10 units. Then we have 10 − 3 units, 9 − 4 tens and 2 − 1 hundreds.

EXAMPLE 4:

3.1 − 0.67

```
    3 . 1 0
  − 0 . 6 7
    2 . 4 3
```

Here it is safer to write in the zero. We can change one of the units into 9 tenths and 10 hundredths. Then we have 10 − 7 hundredths, 10 − 6 tenths and 2 − 0 units.

TOP TIP

There are several ways of showing the 'borrowing' in a subtraction and your teacher will probably have shown you their preferred method. Make sure you can use it by practising and ask for help if you are stuck.

Questions

The answers are at the back of the book.

When answering these questions, you are expected to show clearly all your working, even if you could do these in your head.

2.20 (a) Add 143 to 37 (1)

(b) Subtract 34 from 111 (2)

2.21 (a) Add 5.7 + 6.9 (1)

(b) Subtract 2.48 from 13.5 (2)

2.22 (a) Which number is 5.6 less than 12.3? (1)

(b) What must I add to 11.4 to get 23.2? (2)

Multiplication

EXAMPLE 1:

418 × 7

```
      4  1  8
×           7
   2  9  2  6
      1  5
```

The little 'working' digits may help.

EXAMPLE 2:

76 × 15

```
         7  6
×        1  5
      3  8  0
         3
      7  6  0
   1  1  4  0
         1
```

Multiply 76 by 5 to give 380
The little 'working' digit here is from 5 × 6 = 30
Multiply 76 by 10 to give 760 (remember the zero in the units place) then add 380 and 760
Note the little 'working digits' in the addition.

EXAMPLE 3:

123 × 47

```
         1  2  3
×           4  7
      8  6  1
      1  2
```

7 × 123 is 861

```
   4  9  2  0
      1
```

40 × 123 is 4920 (remember to put the zero in the units place).

```
   5  7  8  1
   1
```

The little 'working' digit in the addition may help.

EXAMPLE 4:

11.5 × 6

```
      1  1  5
×           6
   6  9  0
      3
```

Forget about the point until later.

We now need to put the point in the answer and we will look at two methods for doing this.

Method 1

Notice that there is *one figure* (the 5) to the right of the point in 11.5

There must be *one figure* to the right of the point in the answer.

Therefore the answer is 69.0

Method 2

We can check by looking at the sizes of the numbers being multiplied.

We know that 11 × 6 is 66 and 12 × 6 is 72 so the answer must be between 66 and 72

The answer is 69.0

AIM HIGH

For completeness, we will include one more example, although you would not be expected to do this calculation in the 11+ examination.

EXAMPLE 5:

35.4 × 7.3

```
          3  5  4
   ×         7  3
      1  0  6  2        Forget about the points and proceed as above
            1  1        3 × 354 is 1062

      2  4  7  8  0      70 × 354 is 24 780
         3  2

      2  5  8  4  2
            1
```

We now need to decide where we put the point in the answer.

There are two safe ways of doing this and it is a good idea to use method 1 and then check with method 2!

Method 1
Look at the original calculation and see how many figures there are altogether after the points. In this case there are two, one in each number being multiplied.

There are the same number (in this case two) figures to the right of the point in the answer, so the answer is 258.42

Method 2
Look at the two numbers being multiplied and consider an approximate value for each. In this case we could say 40 and 7 and we know that 40 × 7 is 280 so the answer must be *in the region* of 280

The answer must be 258.42 since it cannot be 25.842 or 2584.2

Largest number

- Choose three consecutive digits, for example 6, 7 and 8.

- Arrange the digits as three multiplications with the digits in order, as shown here.

  67 × 8   86 × 7   78 × 6

- Without doing any calculations, try to guess which will give the smallest result and which will give the largest result.

- Carry out all three multiplications to see if you were correct.

Division

EXAMPLE 1:

215 ÷ 5

$$5 \overline{) 2 \ 1 \ ^1 5}$$ = 4 3

The little 'working' digit may help.
5 goes into 21 four times, remainder 1
and then 5 goes into 15 three times.

This is an example of exact division.

Notice where the little 'working' remainder 1 digit goes.

EXAMPLE 2:

200 ÷ 7

$$7 \overline{) 2 \ ^2 0 \ ^6 0}$$ = 2 8

7 goes into 20 twice, remainder 6 and
then 7 goes into 60 eight times, remainder 4

We can leave the answer as 28 remainder 4

Notice where the little 'working' remainder digits go.

EXAMPLE 3:

Here, we will look at the same division but this time continue to divide until we have an answer to 2 decimal places.

200 ÷ 7

$$7 \overline{) 2 \ ^2 0 \ ^6 0 . ^4 0 \ ^5 0}$$ = 2 8 . 5 7

7 goes into 20 twice, remainder 6,
then 7 goes into 60 eight times, remainder 4, then 7
goes into 40 five times, remainder 5 and finally 7 goes
into 50 seven times with remainder 1

We could carry on but we can write the answer as 28.57 to 2 decimal places.

This is an approximate answer. It is not exact.

EXAMPLE 4:

Now we will look at the same division again but this time leave an exact answer!

200 ÷ 7

$$7 \overline{) 2 \ ^2 0 \ ^6 0 \ ^4}$$ = 2 8

Because we are dividing by 7, the remainder 4 represents 4 sevenths ($\frac{4}{7}$) so we can leave the answer as the mixed fraction $28\frac{4}{7}$ which is exact.

Keep dividing

- Look again at the division Examples 2, 3 and 4 above.

- You will remember that 200 ÷ 7 does not give an integer (whole number) answer.

- Repeat the division in Example 3 but do not stop until you have the result to 10 decimal places. You may be surprised by the result.

- You might like to investigate further.

Questions

The answers are at the back of the book.

When answering these questions, you are expected to show clearly all your working, even if you could do these in your head.

2.23 (a)   Multiply 19 by 8   (2)

    (b)   Multiply 456 by 14   (2)

2.24 (a)   Divide 2045 by 5   (2)

    (b)   Divide 2002 by 7   (2)

2.25 (a)   What is the total cost of 5 DVDs costing £8.75 each?   (2)

    (b)   Share £40 between seven people as best you can.

        (i)   How much will each person receive?   (2)

        (ii)   How much will be left over?   (2)

Multiple choice questions

In these questions you should write the letter of the correct answer.

You may do written calculations if you wish.

2.26 Which of these multiplications has the largest result?   (1)

    A: 24×5 B: 25×4 C: 54×2 D: 42×5 E: 52×4

2.27 How many of these calculations have the answer 8?   (1)

    $3 \times 4 - 4$ $5 + 6 \div 2$ $4 \times 5 - 3$ $5 \times 6 - 2 \times 11$

    $4^2 - 4 \div 2$ $4^2 - 2^3$ $4 \times (5 - 3)$ $(8 - 2)^2 - 7 \times 2^2$

    A: 3   B: 4   C: 5   D: 6   E: 7

2.4 CALCULATOR METHODS

Although calculators may not be used in examinations at this level, you will undoubtedly use them from time to time.

Using a calculator

Calculators (like mobile phones and motor cars) vary; calculators may

- have different key labels
- do calculations in different ways
- be able to do only very simple things
- be capable of doing advanced calculations.

TOP TIP

Your calculator will not make a mistake unless you tell it to!

AIM HIGH

You should

- know what your own calculator can and cannot do
- understand that your calculator will simply follow your instructions, so it is very important to press the right keys in the right order
- have confidence in your ability to use your own calculator
- know when using a calculator is a good idea and when other methods are better and/or quicker
- check your calculation since it is very easy to press the wrong key or forget to press '=' at the appropriate time
- understand how to interpret the calculator display.

To do

Mental method versus calculator challenge!

Look carefully at this shopping bill *without doing any calculation.*

- Get someone to time you, or you could time yourself.
- Using the mental grouping strategy (see page 55), find the total cost. Write this down, and record your time.
- Now see how quickly you can do the addition with a calculator.
- Did you get the same total using mental grouping as you did with the calculator? If not, check to see which is correct.

£0.95
£4.05
£7.50
£2.50
£5.00
£3.70

Interpreting calculator displays

Calculator displays vary but you have probably seen displays like those shown below.

- -4.   negative 4
- 8.5 $8\frac{1}{2}$ (fractions)

                      £8.50   (money)

                      8 hours 30 minutes   (time)

                      8 stones 7 pounds   (weight)

- 3.333333333 $3\frac{1}{3}$ (a recurring decimal)
- 5.999999999   6   (a recurring decimal)

When carrying out real-life calculations it is important to understand what the implications are.

- 4.3   5   (if you are calculating the number of rolls of wallpaper you need)

- 4.3   4   (if you are sharing out sweets and want to see how many each person gets)

The calculator answer is 4.5!

Make up five different real-life problems where the calculator display is 4.5 and in each case give the answer in an appropriate form, with the correct units.

EXAMPLE: John bought a $13\frac{1}{2}$ ft length of wood and cut it into three equal pieces. How long was each piece?

Calculator answer: 4.5 real-life answer: 4 ft 6 inches

Questions

The answers are at the back of the book.

2.28 Sarah divided 2431 by 143 using her calculator. She wrote down the answer as 16

    (i)   Suggest two reasons why Sarah should have realised straight away that her answer was incorrect. (2)

    (ii) What should the answer be? (1)

2.29 Imagine that you are shopping in a supermarket with a £50 note. Use a calculator to keep a record of how much money you have left after buying the items on the list.

First enter 50 and then subtract the cost of each item in turn. You can check how much you have left at any time.

Coffee	2 jars @ £3.23 each
Tea bags	£1.45
Fruit	3 packs @ £2.50
Bread	£1.40
Tomatoes	£1.25
Jam tarts	2 packs @ 95p
Chinese meal for 3	£11.50
Washing powder	£4.90
Muesli	£2.10
Milk	£0.85
Cat food	2 boxes of sachets @ £3.90

How much change can you expect from the £50 note? (3)

Multiple choice questions

For these questions you should use your calculator and write the letter of the correct answer.

2.30 Which of these calculations gives the largest result? (1)

    A: 45^2 B: **39 × 52**   C: **16 811 − 14 785**   D: **1997 + 27**   E: **34 459 ÷ 17**

2.31 What is the result, written correct to 3 significant figures, of the following calculation? (1)

    3.97 + 4.59 × 8.95

    A: 45.05   B: 76.612   C: 45.051   D: 76.6   E: 45.1

2.5 CHECKING RESULTS

AIM HIGH

Checking results is very important, because

- we all make mistakes, no matter how careful we are
- a mistake can have serious and/or costly implications.

TOP TIP

No-one is perfect, so always remember to check your work!

Strategies

Here is a reminder of strategies which can be used.

Common sense

- Check that the result is **odd** or **even** as appropriate (see page 6)
- Check the **units digit** following operations with positive integers.

> EXAMPLE 1: An integer ending in 3 **+** an integer ending in 7 always gives an integer ending in 0 (because 3 + 7 = 10).
>
> EXAMPLE 2: An integer ending in 3 **−** an integer ending in 7 always gives an integer ending in 6 (because 13 − 7 = 6).
>
> EXAMPLE 3: An integer ending in 3 **×** an integer ending in 7 always gives an integer ending in 1 (because 3 × 7 = 21).

Approximations

We can **estimate** (get a rough idea of) the result by using approximations.

> EXAMPLE: If we are multiplying 49 by 61, we know that the result must be about the same as 50 × 60, so it must be fairly close to 3000

Different calculations

Sometimes it may help to do a different calculation to see if the result is the same.

> EXAMPLE: When finding the total cost of items in a shopping list, check by adding the amounts from bottom to top as well as top to bottom.

Inverses

This may be thought of as 'working backwards'.

EXAMPLE: When Tom thought of a number, multiplied by 7 and then subtracted 13, he got 22

What number did he think of?

- In this case, you would probably 'work backwards' to find Tom's number. In other words, you would take the 22, add 13 and then divide by 7 to find that Tom thought of 5

- To check that Tom's number was 5, follow through Tom's operations.

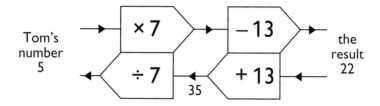

- Start with 5, multiply by 7 (to give 35) and then subtract 13 (to give 22).

Common errors

Common errors, all of which can be avoided with care, include:

Comprehension errors

It may be necessary to read a question more than once in order to understand exactly what is required.

TOP TIP

A check in time saves nine!

- Remember that words like 'not', 'larger', 'negative' and so on can make a big difference to the meaning.

- Take care with signs and symbols such as index numbers, negative signs and brackets.

- Make sure that you know how the answer is to be expressed – for example 'to 3 significant figures', 'in kilometres', 'to the nearest integer'.

Computation errors

These may be multiplication errors. Thorough knowledge of 'tables' is very important (see page 10).

Written errors

These may include:

- failing to set out work in a neat and organised way

EXAMPLE: 4.9 + 10.56	ERROR !!	CORRECT
	4 . 9 1 0 . 5 6 1 4 . 6 5	T U . t h 4 . 9 + 1 0 . 5 6 1 5 . 4 6 1

- forgetting 'carrying digits'

EXAMPLE: 308 + 1975	ERROR !!	CORRECT
	3 0 8 1 9 7 5 2 2 7 3	3 0 8 + 1 9 7 5 2 2 8 3 1　　1

- leaving out zeros or putting in extra zeros

EXAMPLE: Write three metres and seven centimetres in figures.	ERROR !! **3.7 m**	CORRECT 3.07 m

- failing to write the correct units.

EXAMPLE: A rectangle measures 40 mm by 8 mm. What is the area of the rectangle in square centimetres?	ERROR !! **320 mm²**	CORRECT 3.2 cm²

Calculator errors

Things to watch out for include

- using a different calculator – which may do things in a different way
- pressing the wrong key
- failing to press a key when you think you have pressed it
- pressing a key twice by mistake
- failing to press '=' at an appropriate time
- failing to use brackets properly.

You may have made errors when sending texts with a mobile phone. It is just as easy to make similar errors when using your calculator.

Is it wrong?

Look at your answers on a practice examination paper. Study any answer that you got wrong and work through the various checking strategies to see how you could have spotted your error and avoided losing marks.

3 PROBLEM SOLVING

Can you imagine a world without problems? Problems are everywhere! In our daily lives we often need to make decisions – we need to ask questions such as 'What if …?', 'What happens when …?' and so on. We need to find the solutions to problems and this often involves making use of mathematical understanding, knowledge and skills.

3.1 DECISION MAKING

Understanding the problem

Problems in mathematics are best thought of as **puzzles** or **challenges**. They are fun and non-threatening. They are also probably easier to solve than many everyday problems!

Before doing anything else, it is very important to

- understand exactly what the challenge is

- appreciate what *might* be needed in trying to solve the problem, such as drawing instruments, a calculator and so on

- think which general method might best be used:
  - **mental** – entirely in your head
  - **mental with jottings** – perhaps writing down an intermediate result
  - **pencil and paper** – setting out a calculation (such as a long multiplication) on paper, or doing a drawing
  - **practical** – taking measurements, making a model etc
  - **calculator** – only if all other methods are unsuitable!

- be aware of any time limits – for example if the problem is an examination question worth 10% of the marks, then it should be possible to complete it in about 10% of the time allowed for the examination (which would be only 6 minutes in a one hour exam!)

TOP TIP

When is a problem not a problem? When it is maths – maths only has puzzles and challenges!

Deciding on a suitable strategy

AIM HIGH

- Before starting to tackle a problem, it is important to decide on a suitable strategy.
- This is largely a matter of common sense, but you could consider using one, or more, of the following strategies.

Making an organised list (listing all possible outcomes)

EXAMPLE: How many different integers (whole numbers) could you make using these three number cards?

5 **7** **8**

- There are obviously three single-digit numbers: 5, 7 and 8

- There are six two-digit numbers: 57, 58, 75, 78, 85, 87

- There are also six three-digit numbers: 578, 587, 758, 785, 857, 875

- So, altogether, you could make 15 different integers.

Trying a practical approach (drawing diagrams, making models etc)

EXAMPLE: How many diagonals does a regular hexagon have?

● Doing a rough sketch should help you.

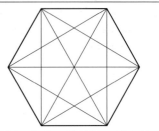

Guessing and checking (trial and improvement)

EXAMPLE: Bertie is thinking of three different positive integers and has given these clues. The product of the numbers is 144 and their sum is 19

What are Bertie's numbers?

● Now, 144 is **4** × 36 and 36 is **2** × **18**, so you could guess that the numbers are **2, 4** and **18**

● Unfortunately, this cannot be correct since the sum of **2, 4** and **18** is 24, not 19

● Your next guess might be 2, 8 and 9 and this would be correct!

Trying a simpler example (trying easier numbers etc)

EXAMPLE: If £50 worth of two pence coins could be placed in a single pile, how high would the pile be? You might make a start by working out how high a pile of five coins would be.

Looking for a pattern

EXAMPLE: Here are some designs made from drinking straws.

Design 1   Design 2   Design 3   Design 4

	Design 1		Design 2		Design 3		Design 4
straws added		8		12		16	
total number of straws	4		12		24		40

How many straws would be needed to make the design with six straws on each edge?

● Design 1 has 4 straws. See how many straws must be added to make design 2.

● We need 8 more straws, making 12 straws altogether.

● To make design 3 we need to add 12 more straws, making a total of 24.

● To make design 4 we need to add 16 more straws, and so on.

● You will see that there is a pattern here: add 8, add 12, add 16, add ….

● We can follow the pattern to find the total number of straws for design 6.

What's the problem?

Think about each of the problems below (and on the following page) and decide which general method (or combination of methods) from the following list might be most suitable.

- mental   **(M)**
- mental with jottings   **(MJ)**
- pencil and paper   **(PP)**
- practical   **(PR)**
- calculator   **(C)**

For each problem, write one or more of the choices **M, MJ, PP, PR** or **C.**

You do not need to solve the problems at the moment!

(i)   What is the cost of 10 books costing £5.99 each?

(ii)   How many diagonals does a regular octagon have?

(iii)   What is the product of 38 and 194?

(iv)   The diagram shows two ways in which two squares and a triangle can be put together to make shapes.

How many different shapes could be made?

(v)   What is the cube root of 100?

(vi)   The diagram on the right shows a series of 'steps' made using matches.

How many matches would be needed to make 10 steps?

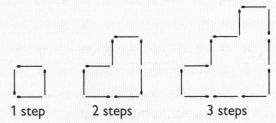

1 step   2 steps   3 steps

(vii)   How many 10 pence coins placed touching in a straight line would stretch 100 metres?

(viii)   Annie, Bill and Clare each think of a positive integer. The sum of their numbers is 25, the difference between the largest and smallest numbers is 5 and the product of the numbers is 528

What are their numbers?

(ix)   What would be the height of a pile of 100 pound coins?

(x)   A, B and C are three consecutive two-digit integers. The sum of the units digits for all three integers is 10, and the sum of the tens digits for the three is 11

What are the three numbers A, B and C?

(xi)   Slobber, the bloodhound, eats one tin of *Wuffalot* every day. A packet of *Crunchit* dog biscuits lasts him 5 days and a sack of *Mixitup* mixer lasts a month. The prices are shown below.

tin of *Wuffalot*   £0.90

packet of *Crunchit*   £1.50

sack of *Mixitup*   £9.50

What would be the approximate cost of feeding Slobber for a year?

(xii)   Keira has started to make a time-line using a scale of 1 millimetre to represent 1 year. How long would her time-line be if she were to go back to the extinction of the dinosaurs, 65 million years ago?

Hint: You might like to start by thinking about the length of the time-line which would represent your lifetime, then perhaps the time since Queen Victoria died in 1901 and then the time since the BC/AD transition, and so on.

(xiii) When a wigglyworm hatches, it consists of its head and a single body segment which has three spots and two bristles.

At the end of each week, a wigglyworm grows another identical body segment.

when hatched   end of one week

How many bristles will a wigglyworm have at the beginning of its 21st week?

You might like to make up a few questions about wigglyworms and try them out on your friends.

(xiv) The regular **hexagon** below has all of its diagonals drawn.

AIM HIGH

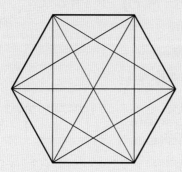

In the diagrams below, two **quadrilaterals** are shaded. How many different **quadrilaterals** are there?

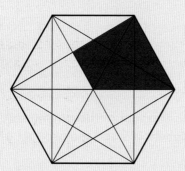   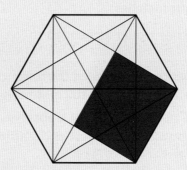

(xv) Which is larger, the area of your foot or the area of your hand?

How to solve the problem

Look again at the problems (i) to (xv) above.

Some of these are fairly straightforward, such as (i), (iii) and (v), but others might make you think harder to find a strategy to be used.

Which strategy (or combination of strategies) might be used in order to solve problems (ii), (iv), (vi), (vii) and (viii)?

Problem solving

Choose two or three of the problems (i) to (xv) and solve them using the method chosen. Did it work well? Was there a better method to choose, do you think? If you do some more revising, choose some others to solve.

3.2 REASONING ABOUT NUMBERS OR SHAPES

When solving puzzles and problems about numbers or shapes, you may need to

- do more thinking than writing

- make use of your knowledge and experience

- make use of a variety of strategies

- make careful observations

- ask yourself questions, such as 'What if …?', 'How about …?'

- be prepared to try a different strategy if you are not succeeding.

TOP TIP

Always question what you see. Just because you see it in black and white does not mean that it is a penguin!

AIM HIGH

Remember to

- search for a solution by trying out ideas of your own

- look for patterns and relationships

- present information and results in a clear and organised way

- check that your results are reasonable.

Try following this advice when tackling the 'Things to do' below and on the following pages.

To do

Geometric puzzle

You will probably be familiar with the tangram puzzle. In the traditional tangram puzzle, a square is cut into seven geometric pieces which are then arranged in different ways to make countless different pictures.

Make up your own, similar, puzzle.

You could start with a regular octagon and divide it into six geometric shapes as shown in this diagram.

Cut out the shapes carefully and then see how many ways you could put them together to make interesting shapes.

Think about the symmetry of each shape you make.

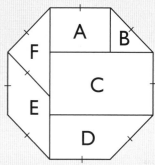

Number challenge game

This is a game for up to nine players but three or four players might be best.

Make a set of cards numbered 1 to 9 and shuffle them. Give each player one card which must not be seen by anyone else. Any spare cards should be kept hidden.

Starting with the player whose name comes first in alphabetical order, the players take turns to ask any one other player a question such as:

'Is your number ….

- less than 5
- a square number
- prime
- odd?'

The questions must have simple 'yes' or 'no' answers.

Suggested rules

- If the answer is 'yes', then the player who asked the question scores 1 point.
- If the answer is 'no', then the player who asked the question loses 1 point.
- If the answer confirms what a player's number is, for example the answer 'yes' to the question 'Is your number 3?' then the player with number 3 is out of the game and the person who asked the question scores 3 points, 4 will score 4 points and so on.
- During the game, if everyone agrees, players could make brief notes, but you may prefer the challenge of trying to remember all the information!
- At the end of the game, the player with the largest score is the winner.
- From time to time, an inexperienced or unlucky player may have a negative score!
- A player must not be asked the same question twice.

Can you devise an effective strategy for playing this game?

Follow a rule to form a number sequence

Choose any two-digit number. Follow the rule *add the digits and then multiply by 2* Write down your answers until the sequence starts to repeat.

Starting with 23, we say (2 + 3) × 2 which gives 10

Then after 10, we say (1 + 0) × 2 which gives 2

Then, after 2, we say 2 × 2 which gives 4 and so on.

EXAMPLES:
$$23 \rightarrow 10 \rightarrow 2 \rightarrow 4 \rightarrow 8 \rightarrow 16 \rightarrow 14 \rightarrow 10$$
$$36 \rightarrow 18 \rightarrow 18$$
$$78 \rightarrow 30 \rightarrow 6 \rightarrow 12 \rightarrow 6$$

What do you notice about the numbers when the sequence starts to repeat? Is there a pattern?

Follow a different rule!

Choose any two-digit number. Follow the rule *'multiply the digits and then add the sum of the digits'* until the sequence starts to repeat or you reach a single-digit number.

EXAMPLES:

48 → 44 (32 + 12) → 24 → 14 → 9

52 → 17 → 15 → 11 → 3

60 → 6   since we have (6 × 0 + 6)

See what you can discover!

Is it divisible by 3?

A **flowchart** can show clearly the order of operations.

Some flowcharts can be very useful in checking or sorting (see also section 6.1 on page 136).

The flowchart below shows how to check if a number is divisible by 3

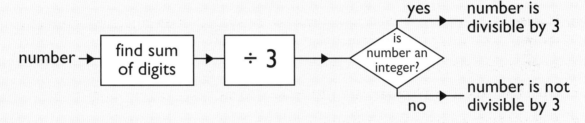

The instructions, in words, would look something like this:

- *Find the sum of the digits of the number*
- *Divide the sum of the digits by 3*
- *Is the result an integer?*
- *If 'yes' then the original number is divisible by 3*
- *If 'no' then the original number is not divisible by 3*

Write down a few integers less than a million at random and check to see how many of them are divisible by 3

What or who is it?

Donna is thinking of a quadrilateral (4-sided plane shape).

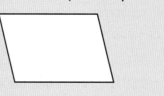

You could follow through the flowchart below, asking Donna the questions, in order to find out what quadrilateral she is thinking of.

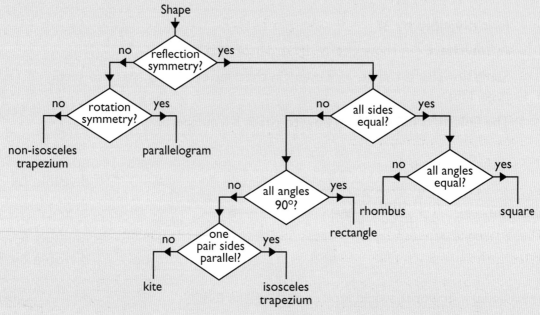

Make up a flowchart to identify the friends in your class. What might be the best first question?

Number guessing game

This is a game you can play with a friend.

Ask your friend to choose a number less than 20, write it down and hide the paper.

See how many questions it takes you to find the number.

Can you devise a strategy which will help you to discover the number in fewer questions?

Design a flowchart, something like the one above, to find the number. See if you can find a way of finding the number in a maximum of five questions.

Questions

The answers are at the back of the book.

3.1 The sum of two numbers is 98

One number is 24 more than the other.

What are the two numbers? (2)

3.2 Robert has four coins in his pocket. He has a total of £1.50

(i)   What are the four coins? (1)

He buys a magazine costing £1.27, handing over three of his coins. The shopkeeper gives him two coins as change.

(ii)   Which coins does the shopkeeper give him? (2)

3.3 Erin has thought of a number and has given these clues.

The number is

● prime

● more than 30 but less than 70

● 2 less than a square number.

What is Erin's number? (3)

3.4 Connor has thought of two numbers.

The product of his numbers is 72

The difference between his numbers is the same as one of his numbers.

What is the sum of Connor's numbers? (3)

3.5 (i)   Shapes P, Q and R have been made by joining together two squares and two triangles, as shown in the diagram on the right.

 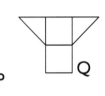

(a)   Which shape has reflection symmetry only? (1)

(b)   Which shape has rotation symmetry only? (1)

(c)   Which shape has no symmetry? (1)

W (ii)   On a square dotted grid or squared paper, show how the same two squares and two triangles can be joined to form the following shapes:

(a)   an isosceles trapezium   S (1)

(b)   a parallelogram   T (1)

(c)   a hexagon   U (1)

(d)   a pentagon   V (2)

3.6 Sean has the three pieces of card shown here.

He arranges the pieces edge to edge to make the following shape.

See how many different shapes you can make using all three pieces. (5)

Note that non-exact edge fits and congruent shapes, as shown below, don't count.

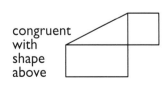

congruent with shape above

3.3 REAL-LIFE MATHEMATICS

Many everyday situations involve mathematics, including:

- shopping
- decorating
- holidays

- cooking
- journeys
- making a model.

A range of mathematical knowledge and skills may be required in these situations. Such skills include:

- measurement
- fractions, decimals and percentages
- compass directions

- money and currency conversions
- ratio and scales
- data tables, graphs etc.

Shopping estimate

We have studied something similar in an earlier chapter, but it is worth looking at this in a slightly different way.

Study Jade's shopping receipt below.

DIET COLA	3.25		STRONG MINTS	1.52
MINERAL WTR	2.47		MERINGUES	1.24
MARGHERITA PZA	1.79		C/TAIL SAUS	1.65
PASTA BAKE	5.00		C/CUP MUSHROOM	0.97
SPONGE CLEANER	0.52		BANANAS 0.780 kg	0.53
DOG FOOD	5.99		M/WAVE RICE	1.69
CAT FOOD	3.49		TOOTHPASTE	1.79
LASAGNE	1.62		BIN LINERS	2.05
DOG TREATS	2.79		PASTA SHELLS	0.85
FRESH MILK	0.89		STEAK MINCE	4.00
MARIS PIPER	1.74		TISSUES	3.98
BROCCOLI 335G	0.97		W/THIN HAM	2.00
SPAGHETTI	0.89		CAT TREATS	0.99
GRATED CHEDDAR	2.23			

As she put the items in the trolley, Jade tried to keep a mental note of the 'running' total cost of the items. Her strategy was to count only whole pounds by rounding the individual prices to the nearest £1

- What total did Jade have in her head at the checkout?

- Use your calculator to find the checkout total.

- How close was Jade to the total shown on the receipt and was her estimate too high or too low?

Make a model

Make a scale model of your bedroom, classroom or garden.

You will need to

- make, and record, real-life measurements
- decide on a suitable scale – such as 1 cm to represent 1 metre
- calculate the scaled down measurements
- make a 'base' showing a bird's eye view of the room or garden
- make scale models of the furniture etc.

Plan a holiday

This could be a plan for a real holiday or an imaginary one!

You will need to

- choose an exciting destination!
- study timetables
- calculate costs
- study currency conversions and so on.

Comparing records

Find out a few interesting facts (such as speeds of animals) and record them as

- positions on number lines, or
- bars in bar charts.

Questions

The answers are at the back of the book.

3.7 Mary buys three bottles of juice costing 86 pence each, three sandwiches costing £1.28 each and a bar of chocolate costing £1.05

How much change will she receive from a £10 note? (3)

3.8 The nutrition information on a chocolate biscuit is shown below.

NUTRITION INFORMATION

mass per	100 g
protein	6.5 g
carbohydrate	63.0 g
fat	25.5 g
per biscuit	
fat	5.1 g

(i)   What percentage of the biscuit is fat? (1)

(ii) What is the mass of a biscuit? (3)

(iii) What is the mass of carbohydrate in one biscuit? (2)

3.9 Iain and Isla are at the seaside. Iain has £2.63 and Isla has 87 pence less than Iain. They decide to put all their money together and buy a large pizza and a bag of chips to share.

Pizza	£3.40
Chips	£0.90

How much money will they have left? (3)

3.10 Samantha wants to make 24 scones for a party.

She has found this recipe:

To make 6 scones	
butter	50 g
flour	225 g
baking powder	3 tsp
salt	½ tsp
caster sugar	30 g
sultanas	50 g
milk	150 ml
eggs	1
preparation time 10 minutes	
cooking time 15 minutes	

(i) Copy the list of ingredients and write the quantities she will need for 24 scones. (4)

(ii) What will the cooking time be? (1)

3.11 Eight friends took part in a marathon to raise money for charity.

The marathon distance is 42.195 kilometres (26 miles 385 yards).

The friends were split into two teams, **A** and **B**. The times taken were recorded in the table below.

Name	Team	Time
Dennis	B	2 h 35 min 43 sec
Blair	A	2 h 48 min 14 sec
Harriet	A	2 h 53 min 29 sec
Angie	B	3 h 04 min 17 sec
Eric	A	3 h 15 min 55 sec
Georgina	B	3 h 23 min 37 sec
Karen	B	3 h 45 min 08 sec
Francis	A	3 h 58 min 44 sec

(i) By how many minutes and seconds did Dennis beat Blair? (2)

To decide which team won, the times of the runners in each team are added.

(ii) Which team has won? (4)

3.12 Colin bought 50 plastic ducks of different colours. The ducks were identical apart from the colour.

Colin numbered the ducks 1 to 50

The table shows the numbers of the ducks of each colour.

Colour	Number of ducks
red	10
green	19
yellow	14
blue	7

(i)   (a) What fraction (in its simplest form) of the ducks was red?   (2)

      (b) What percentage of the ducks was green?   (2)

      (c) What was the ratio of yellow ducks to blue ducks?   (2)

Colin paid £25 for the ducks and sold all of them at 70p each.

(ii) What did Colin pay for each duck?   (2)

(iii) How much money did Colin take from selling the ducks?   (2)

The ducks were dropped at the same time from the middle of a footbridge over a stream. 50 metres downstream, Rachel and Sandra recorded the numbers on the first three ducks to arrive.

(iv) Tommy had bought a green duck because he thought that it was more likely to win. What do you think of this idea?   (2)

The owner of the winning duck won £5, the second won £2 and the third won £1

(v)   (a) What was the total prize money?   (1)

      (b) What was Colin's overall profit to give to charity?   (2)

(vi) What is the probability that the winning duck was *not* red?   (2)

(vii) What is the probability that the number on the winning duck was

      (a) a single-digit number   (2)

      (b) a prime number?   (3)

4 ALGEBRA

Can you imagine a world without algebra? If you think you can, did you know that without algebra there would be no computer graphics? You may be surprised to know that we solve many of life's little problems by making use of algebra, even if we don't realise it! Algebra is a bit like a magic key that opens up opportunities, and helps to take short cuts, in many fields.

4.1 EQUATIONS AND FORMULAE

Word formulae

A **word formula** is a series of instructions to be carried out *in order*.

Puzzles

TOP TIP
Basic algebra is not to be feared! Don't be an ostrich!

- Some of the word formulae you will meet are concerned with puzzles.

AIM HIGH

It is very useful to represent a number that we don't know by a letter or a symbol.

EXAMPLE 1: *'Annabel thought of a number, multiplied by 2 and then added 5'*

- We can represent this word formula by a flowchart.

$$a \rightarrow \boxed{\times 2} \rightarrow \boxed{+ 5} \rightarrow$$

- We do not, so far, know what number Annabel thought of, so we have represented her number by the letter a.

- If Annabel thought of 6, then we would find the result by doing the calculation
  $6 \times 2 + 5 \rightarrow 17$

EXAMPLE 2: *'Brian thought of a number, added 5 and then multiplied by 2'*

- We can represent this word formula by a flowchart.

$$b \rightarrow \boxed{+ 5} \rightarrow \boxed{\times 2} \rightarrow$$

TOP TIP
Notice that although Annabel and Brian chose the same number, 6, the results are different because the operations + 5 and × 2 were done in a different order. (It may be a good idea to look again at BIDMAS in section 2.1 on page 52)

- We do not know what number Brian thought of, so we have represented his number by the letter b.

- If Brian chose the same number as Annabel, 6, then we could find Brian's result by doing the calculation
  $(6 + 5) \times 2 \rightarrow 22$

EXAMPLE 3: *'Calum thought of a number, subtracted 4 and then multiplied by 3*

The result was 27'

- This time, we are told what the result is, but we do not yet know Calum's number.

- We can represent this word formula by a flowchart.

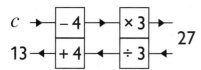

$$c \rightarrow \boxed{- 4} \rightarrow \boxed{\times 3} \rightarrow \quad 27$$
$$13 \leftarrow \boxed{+ 4} \leftarrow \boxed{\div 3} \leftarrow$$

- We can work backwards, using a reverse flowchart to find out what Calum's number was.

Number puzzles

Write a 'think of a number' puzzle similar to the examples on page 82 and then draw a flowchart to represent it. Make up a few 'think of a number' puzzles to try on your friends.

Number puzzle game

Jo has drawn a two-stage machine to illustrate her puzzle.

Keira has invented a game, based on Jo's machine.

She has drawn a blank machine.

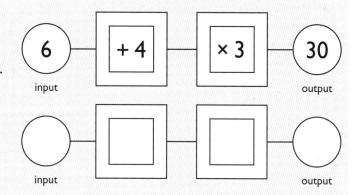

She has cut out the following 'pieces'.

Dark labels:

Light labels:

Input/output numbers:

Rules

- The pieces are put in three separate piles. The piles are shuffled and placed face down.
- Players take it in turns.
- A player takes one piece from each pile and places the pieces on the machine so that the missing input or output is the *largest* possible number (integer or, in some cases, fraction).

There are four possible arrangements for the three pieces.

pieces picked

EXAMPLE: In this example, the first arrangement gives the largest missing number.

- If the opposing player can find an arrangement to make a higher missing input or output, then he 'steals' the turn.
- The player records that number (integer or fraction) as a score for the turn.

In this example, the player would score 4

- The game continues until an agreed winning score is reached.

You might like to modify the game by making more pieces.

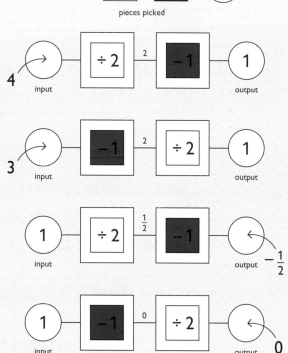

Conversions

- Some word formulae help us to convert one unit to another.

- The result may only be approximate but the operation is '**fixed**' (that is, it is always the same).

> EXAMPLE:
>
> - The word formula below will convert a distance in miles to the *approximate* equivalent distance in kilometres.
>
>   '*Multiply by 8 and then divide by 5*'
>
> - We can represent this word formula by a flowchart.
>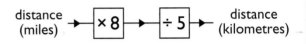

- In some conversion situations the operation can vary. The pounds to dollars conversion rate varies from day to day so we would need to check to see what the current rate is before using a formula.

Conversions

Decide on a 'fixed' conversion situation, such as converting pints to litres. Don't worry if the conversion gives only an approximate result.

Write the word formula and then draw a flowchart to illustrate it.

Value of silver

Decide on a 'variable' conversion situation, such as grams of silver to the value of the item. Find out what the current rate is.

Write the word formula and then draw a flowchart to illustrate it.

Calculations

- Some word formulae help us to perform useful calculations.

> EXAMPLE 1: The word formula below will calculate the total cost C, in pounds, of n pencils which are priced at 11 pence each.
>
> '*Multiply the number of pencils by 11 and then divide by 100*'
>
> We can represent this word formula by a flowchart. $n \rightarrow \boxed{\times\ 11} \rightarrow \boxed{\div\ 100} \rightarrow C$
>
> We could write this as a formula, using symbols, as $C = \left[\dfrac{11}{100}\right]n$
>
> EXAMPLE 2: The word formula below will calculate the perimeter of a rectangle.
>
> '*Add the length to the width and then multiply by 2*'
>
> We can represent this word formula by a flowchart.
>
> We could write this as a formula using symbols as
>
> $P = (l + w) \times 2$ or $P = 2(l + w)$

Flowcharts representing functions

- A simple flowchart can represent a **function**.

- A function is a rule for changing one number into another (see section 4.2, page 89).

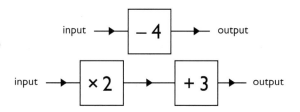

Expressions

> EXAMPLE 1: *'Annabel thought of a number, multiplied by 2 and then added 5'*
>
> - We can replace this word formula by an **expression**, where we will represent Annabel's number by the letter a since we do not know what it is.
>
> - The expression is **$2a + 5$**
>
> EXAMPLE 2: *'Brian thought of a number, added 5 and then multiplied by 2'*
>
> - We can write this word formula as the expression **$2(b + 5)$** where b is Brian's number.

Substitution

- We may sometimes be told the values of unknown numbers.

- We can **substitute** the values in an expression.

> EXAMPLE 1: If we are told that Annabel thought of the number 7, then the **value** of the expression $2a + 5$ is 19 since we have $2 \times 7 + 5$
>
> EXAMPLE 2: If Brian thought of the number 4, then the value of the expression $2(b + 5)$ is 18 since we have $2 \times (4 + 5)$

Equations

- An **equation** is an expression with an equals sign in it.

- In Calum's case (on page 82) we are told what the result was.

  'Calum thought of a number, subtracted 4 and then multiplied by 3

  The result was 27'

- We can replace this word formula by the equation   **$3(c - 4) = 27$**

Solving equations

- Equations can be **solved** to find the unknown number.

EXAMPLE 1:

$$a + 3 = 7$$
$$a = 4 \quad \text{(taking 3 from both sides of the equation to 'keep the balance')}$$

EXAMPLE 2:

$$b - 4 = 12$$
$$b = 16 \quad \text{(adding 4 to both sides)}$$

EXAMPLE 3:

$$4c = 12$$
$$c = 3 \quad \text{(dividing both sides by 4)}$$

- Sometimes we may need more than a single, simple step.

EXAMPLE 4:

$$2d + 3 = 7$$
$$2d = 4 \quad \text{(taking 3 from both sides)}$$
$$d = 2 \quad \text{(dividing both sides by 2)}$$

EXAMPLE 5:

$$2(e + 3) = 16$$
$$2e + 6 = 16 \quad \text{(multiplying out the bracket; } 2 \times e \text{ plus } 2 \times 3\text{)}$$
$$2e = 10 \quad \text{(taking 6 from both sides)}$$
$$e = 5 \quad \text{(dividing both sides by 2)}$$

Questions

The answers are at the back of the book.

4.1 Find the unknown number in each case.

(i) Ethan is 11 years old and is 4 years younger than Fiona.

   $11 + 4 = ☺$

   How old is Fiona? (1)

(ii) A regular hexagon has a perimeter of 42 cm.

   $6 × ▼ = 42$

   What is the length of a side of the hexagon? (1)

4.2 (a) Find the numbers represented by the symbols in these equations.

      (i) $7 + ☼ = 23$ (1)

      (ii)   ♣ − 8 = 7 (1)

      (iii) $9 × ♦ = 36$ (1)

      (iv) $5 × ♣ × 7 = 140$ (1)

      (v) $37 + 44 = ✪ × 9$ (2)

(b) Find the numbers represented by the letters in these equations.

      (i) $a + 5 = 12$ (1)

      (ii) $b − 6 = 6$ (1)

      (iii) $4c = 20$ (1)

      (iv) $3d − 4 = 2$ (2)

      (v) $3(e − 4) = 9$ (3)

4.3 (a) Geoff has thought of a number. When he subtracts 5 he gets 7

      What is Geoff's number? (1)

(b) Helen has thought of a number. When she adds 9 she gets 23

      What is Helen's number? (1)

(c) Lisa has thought of a number. When she multiplies it by 3 she gets 27

      What is Lisa's number? (1)

(d) Jim has thought of a number. When he divides it by 7 he gets 5

      What is Jim's number? (1)

(e) Ken thought of a number. He multiplied it by 7 and then added 6

      (i)   Write an expression to represent this. **AIM HIGH** (1)

      (ii) If Ken thought of the number 5, what was the result? (1)

(f) Jo thought of a number. She added 4 and then multiplied by 3

      (i)   Write an expression to represent this. (1)

      (ii) If Jo thought of the number 6, what was the result? (1)

(g) Three friends, Anne, Bella and Clare each thought of a number.

      (i)   Write an expression for the sum of their numbers. (1)

      (ii) If Anne's number was 2, Bella's number was 5 and Clare's number was 7, what was the sum of their numbers? (1)

4.2 SEQUENCES AND FUNCTIONS

Sequences

- A **sequence** is a list of numbers which follow a **rule** or **pattern**.

AIM HIGH

- A **function** is a rule for changing one number into another.

EXAMPLES:

× 3   − 5

We looked at a few sequences in section 1.1 (see page 7).

EXAMPLE 1:

- For the sequence   1, 5, 9, 13, 17, …   the rule is 'add 4'.

- To produce the sequence, we apply the rule (function) over and over again.

$$\begin{array}{ccc} & \mathbf{+\,4} & \\ 1 & \rightarrow & 5 \\ 5 & \rightarrow & 9 \\ 9 & \rightarrow & \ldots \end{array}$$ and so on.

- Alternatively, we could write this as

$$1 \;\xrightarrow{+\,4}\; 5 \;\xrightarrow{+\,4}\; 9 \;\xrightarrow{+\,4}\; 13 \;\xrightarrow{+\,4}\; 17 \;\xrightarrow{+\,4}\;$$ and so on.

EXAMPLE 2:

- For the sequence   64, 32, 16, 8, 4, …   the rule is 'divide by 2'.

- To produce the sequence, we apply the rule (function) over and over again.

$$\begin{array}{ccc} & \mathbf{\div\,2} & \\ 64 & \rightarrow & 32 \\ 32 & \rightarrow & 16 \\ 16 & \rightarrow & \ldots \end{array}$$ and so on.

Function machines

- A **function machine** consists of one or more functions, in order, with an **input** and **output** of numbers.

- An **input** is a number which 'goes into' a function machine.

- An **output** is a number which 'comes out of' a function machine.

EXAMPLE 1:

- This function machine consists of the single function 'add 5'.

input	→	**+ 5**	→	output
1		→		6
7		→		12
23		→		28
⁻3		→		2
0		→		5

EXAMPLE 2:

- This function machine consists of two functions, 'multiply by 2' and 'add 3'.

input	→	**× 2**	→		**+ 3**	→	output
1		→	2	→			5
7		→	14	→			17
23		→	46	→			49
⁻3		→	⁻6	→			⁻3
0		→	0	→			3

- It is sometimes helpful to write down the intermediate result after the first operation (in this case multiplying by 2).

EXAMPLE 3:

- This function machine consists of the same two functions as the machine in Example 2 but the order of the two functions is reversed.

input	→	**+ 3**	→		**× 2**	→	output
1		→	4	→			8
7		→	10	→			20
23		→	26	→			52
⁻3		→	0	→			0
0		→	3	→			6

- Notice what a difference the order of operations makes!

- The pair of numbers (input, output) is called an **ordered pair**. The input number always comes first.

EXAMPLE 4:

- Consider this simple function machine.

input	→	**− 1**	→	output
1		→		0
2		→		1
3		→		2
4		→		3

- The ordered pairs (input, output) are:

  (1, 0), (2, 1), (3, 2), (4, 3), ….

- This is a sequence of ordered pairs.

Exploring number patterns

You may remember these patterns which we looked at in section 3.1

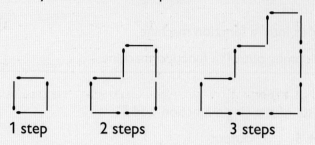

| 1 step | 2 steps | 3 steps |

To get from one step pattern to the next, we add 4 matches so we could consider the function machine:

number of matches in last step pattern	+ 4	number of matches in next step pattern
4	→	8
8	→	12
12	→	16
16	→	20

The next sequence consists of the numbers of straws.

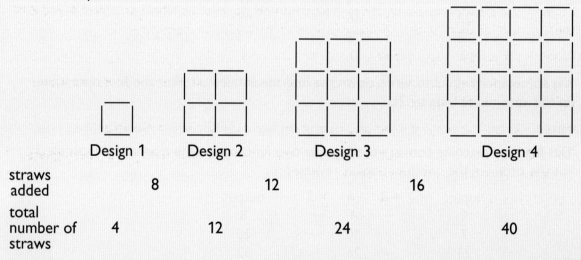

	Design 1	Design 2	Design 3	Design 4
straws added		8	12	16
total number of straws	4	12	24	40

To get from one design to the next, we added 8 straws, then 12 straws, then 16 straws and so on, so we could consider the function machine:

number of straws added last time	+ 4	number of straws to be added
8	→	12
12	→	16
16	→	20
20	→	24

Ask questions such as 'What if…?', 'Why?', 'What happens when…?' and look for patterns in the numbers. Look for rules which may be useful. Make predictions and see what other number patterns you can find.

Function machine game – a game for two players

You will need two sets of 6 function machine labels, as shown below.

Set 1: | + 1 | | + 2 | | + 3 | | − 1 | | − 2 | | − 3 |

Set 2: | × 2 | | × 3 | | × 4 | | × 5 | | × 6 | | ÷ 2 |

You will also need some sheets of paper with a function machine like the one below.

Function machine

input → | A | → | B | → output

....
....
....
....

The rules

- Each player needs a copy of the function machine.

- The two sets of labels are shuffled.

- Player 1 takes two labels, one from each set, and keeps everything hidden from player 2.

- Player 1 chooses the order of the two functions and places the labels on boxes A and B of the function machine, which should of course remain hidden from player 2!

- Player 2 suggests an input number.

- Player 1 works out what the output is, writing on his copy of the function machine, and tells player 2 what the output is.

- Player 2 keeps a record of input and output on her copy of the function machine.

- Player 2 suggests another input number, and the game continues until player 2 can guess correctly what functions are on boxes A and B.

You may like to invent a scoring system.

Questions

The answers are at the back of the book.

4.4 Katie has made a machine which adds 4 to every input number.

    (i)   What will be the output if

        (a)   Katie puts 2 into the machine   (1)

        (b)   Katie puts 9 into the machine?   (1)

    (ii) If 4 comes out of the machine, which number did Katie put in?   (2)

input → | + 4 | → output

4.5 Liam has made a machine.

His machine multiplies by 3 and then subtracts 5

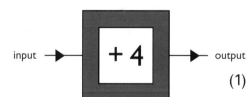

input → | × 3 | → | − 5 | → output

    (i)   What will be the output if

        (a)   Liam puts in 3   (1)

        (b)   he puts in 7?   (1)

    (iii) If ⁻2 comes out, which number did Liam put in?   (2)

4.6 (a) Moira has made a machine which adds 2 and then multiplies by 5

Moira put in a number and 45 came out. What number did Moira put in? (2)

(b) Niall's machine adds 4 and then divides by 2

He put in a number and $3\frac{1}{2}$ came out! What number did Niall put in? (2)

4.7 Write

(a) the function involved

(b) the next two numbers

in each of these sequences.

    (i)   3, 6, 9, 12, 15, ... (1)

    (ii) 1, 2, 4, 8, 16, ... (1)

    (iii) 37, 33, 29, 25, 21, ... (2)

    (iv) 15, 12, 9, 6, 3, ... (2)

4.8 Write the next two numbers in each of these sequences.

    (i)   1, 2, 4, 7, 11, 16, ... (2)

    (ii) 1, 3, 4, 7, 11, 18, ... (2)

4.9 Suggest three multiplication function machines that could produce all these outputs.

    12   18   36   54   78   240 (2)

4.10 Look at these arrangements of straws.

arrangement   arrangement   arrangement
    1   2   3

(i) Sketch arrangement 4 (1)

(ii) How many straws would be needed for

    (a) arrangement 5 (1)

    (b) arrangement 8? (2)

Oliver suggests that you could find the number of straws needed for an arrangement simply by multiplying the number of squares by 3 and then adding 1

(iii) Does Oliver's idea give the correct number of straws for arrangement 5 and arrangement 8? (1)

(iv) Draw a function machine to represent Oliver's idea. (3)

(v) Use Oliver's idea to find how many straws would be needed for

    (a) arrangement 100 (1)

    (b) arrangement 1000 (1)

Pippa suggests that it should be possible to find, quite easily, the largest arrangement which could be made with a million straws! She suggests putting Oliver's function machine into reverse.

(vi) Using Pippa's idea, or otherwise, find the largest arrangement which could be made with a million straws. (2)

4.3 GRAPHS

The co-ordinate grid

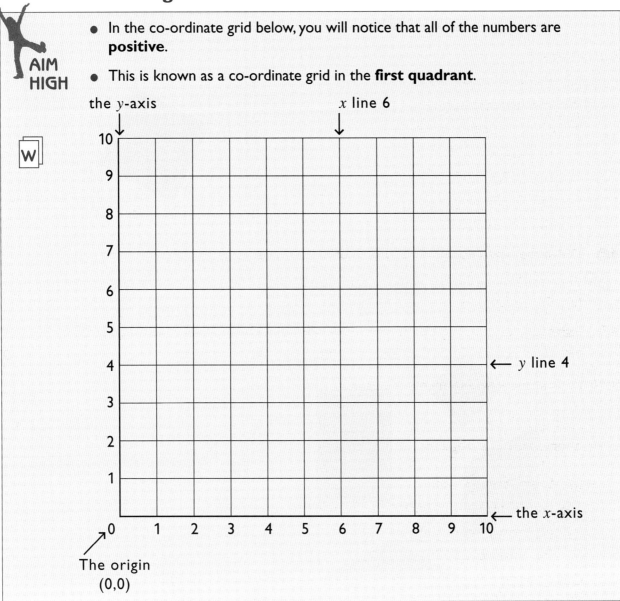

AIM HIGH

W

- In the co-ordinate grid below, you will notice that all of the numbers are **positive**.
- This is known as a co-ordinate grid in the **first quadrant**.

the y-axis

x line 6

← y line 4

← the x-axis

The origin (0,0)

The grid

- The **grid** consists of vertical lines (the **x lines**) and horizontal lines (the **y lines**).
- The **x-axis** (which is y line 0) tells you the number of the x line.
- The **y-axis** (which is x line 0) tells you the number of the y line.
- The **origin** is the point where the axes cross.

Points

- A **point** lies at the intersection of an x line and a y line.
- The **co-ordinates** of a point are the ordered pair of numbers (x, y).
- The origin has co-ordinates $(0, 0)$.

Shapes drawn on a grid

● The square on the grid (right) has its vertices at the following points:

A (2, 0), B (4, 1), C (3, 3) and D (1, 2).

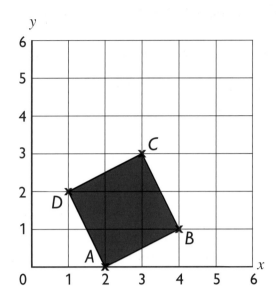

To do

Find the shapes

You may be familiar with the game 'battleships'. This game for two players is similar.

Each player needs a blank copy of the co-ordinate grids shown below.

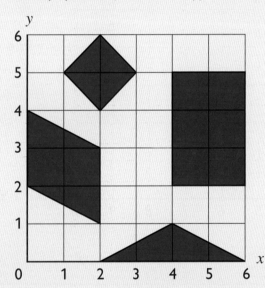 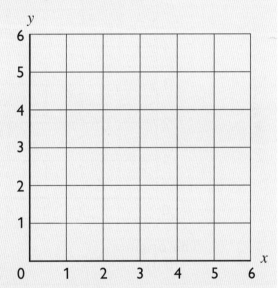

The diagram above shows the start of a game.

The rules

● Each player draws four shapes on a copy of the left-hand grid:
   ● square ● rectangle ● parallelogram ● isosceles triangle.

● The shapes must not overlap and all vertices must be at grid points.

● Player 1 calls out a co-ordinate pair, such as (3, 2).

● Player 2 informs player 1 if this point lies on the edge of, or inside, one of the shapes and what the shape is. For example, player 2 might say

   ● 'vertex of square' ● 'inside parallelogram' ● 'on edge of isosceles triangle' ● 'miss!'

● Both players keep a record.

● Players take it in turns to call out a co-ordinate pair.

● The game continues until the positions of all of a player's shapes have been discovered.

Functions represented on a grid

AIM HIGH

- Consider this simple function machine.

input	→	**+ 3**	→	output
1		→		4
2		→		5
3		→		6
4		→		7
x		→		y $(x + 3)$

- The ordered pairs, (input, output), can be considered as (x, y) co-ordinates, as shown: $(1, 4), (2, 5), (3, 6), (4, 7), \ldots$

- We can plot these ordered pairs on a co-ordinate grid.

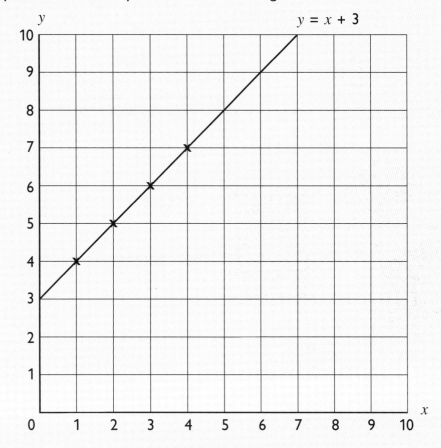

- The line drawn through these points is called the **graph** of the function.

- We could write the function as a word formula '*think of a number and add 3 to get the result*'

  ○ or we could write it in shorthand as '*input + 3 → output*'

  ○ or '*x + 3 → y*'

  ○ or '*x + 3 = y*'

- We could turn things round slightly and write '*we get out 3 more than we started with*'

  ○ or '*output is 3 more than input*'

  ○ or '*y = x + 3*'

x and *y* challenge!

Remember that

- the *x* lines are vertical and the *y* lines are horizontal

- the axes tell you which *x* line or *y* line you are on.

You need a copy of the co-ordinate grid on page 93.

You need a coin which is 'tossed' to decide on *x* line or *y* line

- 'heads'   move along the *x* line

- 'tails'   move along the *y* line.

You need a spinner, like the one shown
to decide how many places are to be moved.

Each player needs a different coloured pencil.

Rules

- Players all start at the origin (0, 0).

- Players take it in turns to toss the coin and spin the spinner and draw their line accordingly.

EXAMPLE:

- 'heads' and 2   the player draws a line 2 units along the *x* line

- 'tails' and 3   the player draws a line 3 units along the *y* line

The first player to reach the edge of the grid is the winner.

The diagram below shows a game for two players in progress.

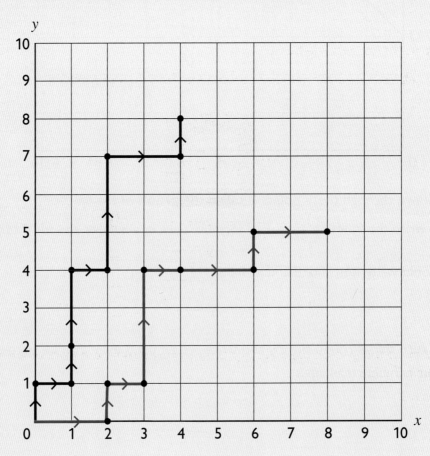

x and y challenge part 2!

You could use the spinner and 4-quadrant co-ordinate grid below to play a similar, more advanced game to the one on page 96.

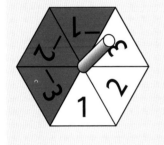

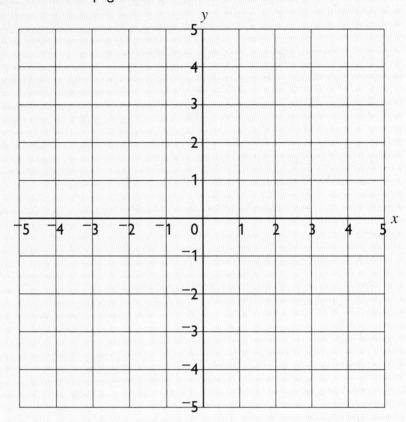

Questions

The answers are at the back of the book.

4.11 (i) Copy and complete the table of outputs for this function machine. (2)

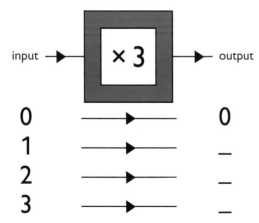

(ii) On copy of the grid on page 93, plot points representing the pairs of input and output numbers. (2)

4.12 A function machine has produced the ordered pairs of numbers plotted on this grid.

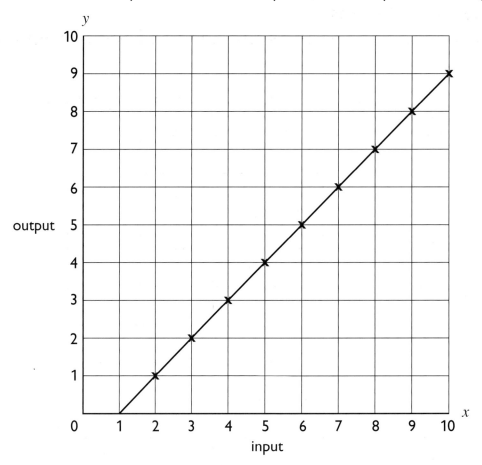

(i)   What would be the output for input 2? (1)

(ii) What would be the input for output 2? (1)

(iii) Copy and complete the word equation which describes the function.

Output = … (2)

4.13 (i)   On another copy of the grid on page 93, plot the points A (3, 2), B (6, 2), C (7, 4) and D (4, 4). (2)

(ii) Join the points, in order, to form the shape ABCD. (1)

(iii) What shape is ABCD? (1)

(iii) What are the co-ordinates of the mid-point of ABCD? (1)

4.14 (i)   Quentin's function machine adds 3 to the input number.

(a) Copy and complete this list of ordered pairs of (input, output) numbers:

(0, 3), (1, …), (2, …), (3, …), (4, …) (2)

(b) Plot these as points on another blank copy of the grid on page 93. (2)

(c) Draw, and label, the graph of Quentin's function. (1)

(ii) Rebecca's function machine multiplies the input number by 2.

(a) Copy and complete this list of ordered pairs of (input, output) numbers:

(0, 0), (1, …), (2, …), (3, …), (4, …) (2)

(b) Plot these as points on the same grid you used in part (i). (2)

(c) Draw, and label, the graph of Rebecca's function. (1)

4.15 Xerxes and Yorick have each thought of a positive integer less than 10

The sum of their numbers is 15

We could write this as $x + y = 15$ where x is Xerxes' number and y is Yorick's number.

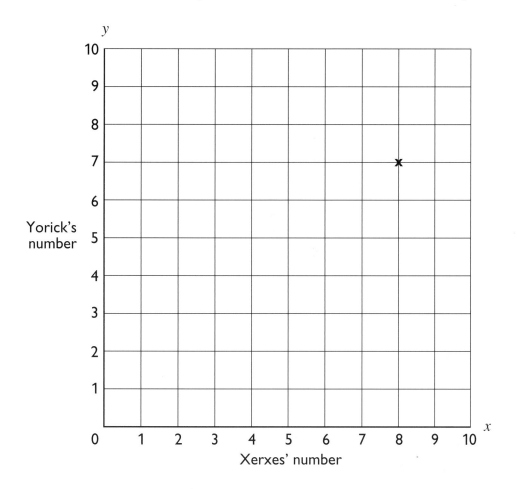

On the diagram, one possibility for the two numbers is shown by a cross.

Copy and complete the diagram to show all of the other possibilities. (3)

5 SHAPE, SPACE AND MEASURES

Can you imagine a world without shape, space and measures? Since everything that exists has shape and occupies space, this would be quite difficult! In mathematics we usually restrict our thinking to plane shapes, solid shapes, symmetry, angles, patterns, maps, scale drawings and so on. Measures have been an important feature of everyday life since ancient times.

5.1 MEASURES

Measurement of length and distance

Instruments include

- **rulers** to measure a straight line drawn on a piece of paper

- **tapes** to measure round your waist

- **trundle wheels** to measure a distance around a running track.

Units include

- **metric** units: millimetre (mm), centimetre (cm), metre (m), kilometre (km)

			Think of:
1 km	=	1000 m	the distance you could walk in 10 minutes
1 m	=	100 cm	
1 cm	=	10 mm	

- **Imperial** units: inch (in), foot (ft), yard (yd), mile

			Think of:
1 mile	=	1760 yd	the distance you could walk in 15 minutes
1 yd	=	3 ft	a normal adult pace when measuring a distance
1 ft	=	12 in	your 30 cm ruler!

AIM HIGH

Unit conversions (all approximate)

Conversion	or, written more simply	or
kilometres → **× 5** → **÷ 8** → miles	kilometres → **× 0.62** → miles	kilometres → **÷ 1.6** → miles
kilometres ← **÷ 5** ← **× 8** ← miles	kilometres ← **÷ 0.62** ← miles	kilometres ← **× 1.6** ← miles

metres → **× 1.1** → yards   centimetres → **× 0.4** → inches

metres ← **÷ 1.1** ← yards   centimetres ← **÷ 0.4** ← inches

Useful conversions to remember

8 km → 5 miles   30 cm → 1 foot

1 m → 40 inches   2.5 cm → 1 inch

Measurement of mass

Instruments include

- weighing scales where an unknown mass is compared to known masses (some kitchen scales)

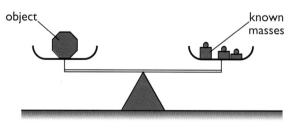

object   known masses

- spring balances where the unknown mass stretches (or compresses) a spring (most bathroom scales and some kitchen scales)

- home-made microbalances for measuring very small masses (see Appendix 1, page 154).

Units include

- **metric** units: milligram (mg), gram (g), kilogram (kg), tonne (t)

			Think of:
1 tonne	=	1000 kg	a small car
1 kg	=	1000 g	a bag of sugar
1 g	=	1000 mg	a small sweet or a small paper clip or a drawing pin
1 mg			a grain of sugar

AIM HIGH

- **Imperial** units: ounce (oz), pound (lb), stone (st), hundredweight (cwt), ton

			Think of:
1 ton	=	160 stones	a small car
1 stone	=	14 lb	
1 lb	=	16 oz	a tub of butter
1 oz			a £5 coin

Useful conversions to remember

6.35 kg	→	1 stone
1 kg	→	2.2 lb
450 g	→	1 lb

Microbalance

Make a **microbalance** (see Appendix 1, page 154) and use it to find the masses of very small objects.

Sports equipment

Use the internet to find the masses of the balls used in soccer, rugby, tennis, hockey, volleyball, golf, netball and basketball.

Questions

The answers are given at the back of the book.

5.1 (a) A snake has length 3.05 metres. Write this measurement in
  (i) centimetres (1)
  (ii) millimetres (1)
  (iii) feet and inches. (2)

 (b) Walter's mass is 45 kilograms.

 Write Walter's mass in
  (i) grams (1)
  (ii) pounds (2)
  (iii) stones and pounds. (1)

Measurement of capacity and volume

Instruments include

- measuring spoons (usually 5 ml, used for doses of medicine etc)
- measuring cups or jugs (used in cooking)
- measuring cylinders (used for accurate measurements in science).

Units include

- **metric** units: millilitre (ml), litre (l)

			Think of:
1 litre	=	1000 ml	a carton of juice
1 millilitre			a medicine spoon (5 ml)

- **Imperial** units: gallon (gal), pint (pt), fluid ounce (fl oz)

			Think of:
1 gallon	=	8 pints	a small bucket (such as an ice bucket)
1 pint	=	20 fluid ounces	a pint of milk
1 fluid ounce			a small egg cup

The following unofficial, *very approximate*, equivalents might be useful, although these are not often needed:

1 tablespoon	→	0.5 fluid ounce
1 mug	→	8 fluid ounces

Useful conversions to remember

AIM HIGH	1 litre	→	1.75 pints
	1 gallon	→	4.5 litres

How heavy is it?

- Find out as much as you can about **measures** in everyday use.
- Gain experience of knowing what various **masses** feel like, including:
  1 kilogram, 500 grams, 1 stone, 1 pound, 1 ounce.
- Practise guessing the masses of various items, such as a bag of potatoes, a bucket of sand, a cat, your little brother or sister.
- Gain experience of knowing what various **capacities** look like, including:
  1 litre, 250 millilitres, 1 gallon, 1 pint.

Measurement of temperature

Instruments include

- mercury thermometers (used under the armpit)
- plastic thermometer strips (used on the forehead)
- electronic thermocouples (used in kitchens to check temperature of food).

Units include

- degrees Celsius (°C)
- degrees Fahrenheit (°F).

Freezer or ice compartment in fridge	⁻18 °C	0 °F
Fridge	3 to 5 °C	37 to 41 °F
Human body temperature	37 °C	98 °F

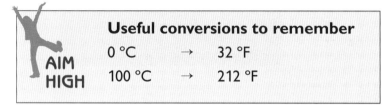

Useful conversions to remember

0 °C	→	32 °F
100 °C	→	212 °F

Measurement of area

- Areas are usually calculated rather than measured.

Units include

- **metric** units: square centimetre (cm²), square metre (m²), hectare (ha), square kilometre (km²)

1 cm

1 cm   area 1 cm²

			Think of:
1 km²	=	100 ha	a square of side 1 km on a map
1 ha	=	10 000 m²	an international rugby pitch
1 m²	=	10 000 cm²	a square of side 1 m
1 cm²			a finger-nail

- **Imperial** units: square inch, square foot, square yard, square mile

	Think of:
1 acre	a soccer pitch
1 square inch	a large letter postage stamp

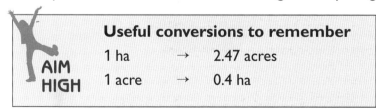

Useful conversions to remember

1 ha	→	2.47 acres
1 acre	→	0.4 ha

Calculation of perimeters

- The **perimeter** of a shape is the distance around the edge.

- The perimeter of a square of side 3 cm is 12 cm (4 sides, each of length 3 cm).

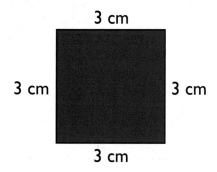

3 cm

3 cm   3 cm

3 cm

- The perimeter of a rectangle measuring 6 cm by 2 cm could be calculated by adding
6 + 2 + 6 + 2 = 16 cm or we could say that it will be 2(6 + 2) cm.

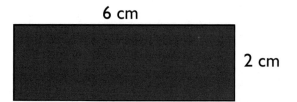

6 cm

2 cm

We can write a **formula** for the perimeter of a rectangle as

$P = 2(l + w)$

where P is the perimeter, l is the length and w is the width of the rectangle.

- We can find the perimeter of a compound plane shape made of rectangles.

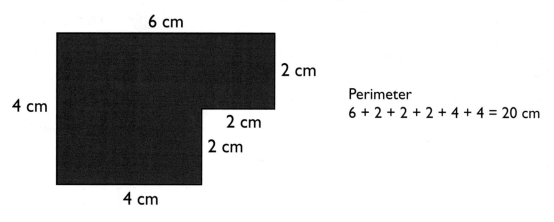

6 cm

2 cm

4 cm

2 cm

2 cm

4 cm

Perimeter
6 + 2 + 2 + 2 + 4 + 4 = 20 cm

- The perimeter of a regular hexagon of side 2 cm is 12 cm (6 sides, each of length 2 cm).

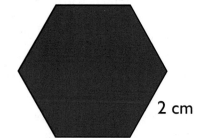

2 cm

Calculation of areas

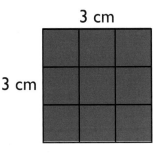

3 cm

3 cm

- **The area of a plane shape** is a measure of the two-dimensional space inside it.

- We can find the area by counting centimetre squares inside the shape.

- The area of the square on the right is 9 cm².

- We could calculate the area by saying that there are 3 rows of 3 squares (3 × 3).

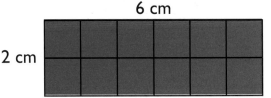

6 cm

2 cm

- The area of this rectangle is 12 cm².

- We could calculate the area by saying that there are 2 rows of 6 squares (2 × 6).

AIM HIGH

We can write a formula for the area of a rectangle as

$A = l × w$

where A is the area, l is the length and w is the width of the rectangle.

- We can find the area of a compound plane shape made up of rectangles.

TOP TIP

This area of maths is not as tricky as it may seem!

- We could add the areas of the smaller rectangles or subtract the area of a smaller rectangle from a larger rectangle.

- To find the area of a regular hexagon, or any other shape, we could count centimetre squares inside it.

- The areas of the triangles below are all 4 cm² (half the area of the rectangle in which they fit).

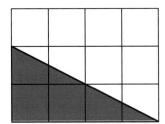 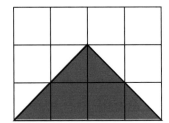 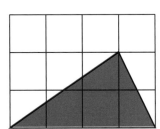

AIM HIGH

The area of each triangle is half of the product of the base and the height.

Calculation of volumes

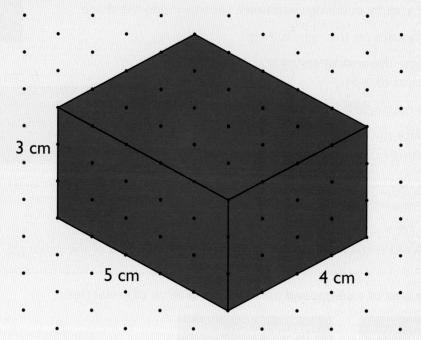

- **The volume of a solid shape** is a measure of the three-dimensional space inside it.

- The diagram above shows a cuboid measuring 5 cm × 4 cm × 3 cm made from centimetre cubes.

- There are 20 (5 × 4) centimetre cubes in each layer and there are 3 layers, so there are 60 centimetre cubes altogether.

- We write the volume as 60 cm³.

  We can write a formula for the volume of a cuboid as $V = l \times w \times h$ where V is the volume, l is the length, w is the width and h is the height of the cuboid.

Questions

The answers are at the back of the book.

5.2 A rectangle measures 8 cm by 6 cm. What is

   (i)   its perimeter   (1)

   (ii) its area?   (1)

5.3 The three models shown below have been made from centimetre cubes.

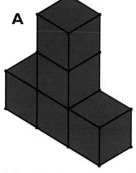
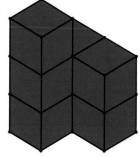

What is the volume of

   (i)   model A   (2)

   (ii) model B   (2)

   (iii) model C?   (2)

Measuring and recording time

We will just consider seconds, minutes and hours.

Remember

- 1 hour   =   60 minutes

- $\frac{1}{2}$ hour (0.5 h)   =   30 minutes

- $\frac{1}{3}$ hour   =   20 minutes

- $\frac{1}{4}$ hour (0.25 h)   =   15 minutes

- $\frac{1}{5}$ hour (0.2 h)   =   12 minutes

- $\frac{1}{10}$ hour (0.1 h)   =   6 minutes

- $\frac{1}{60}$ hour   =   1 minute

- 1 minute   =   60 seconds

The 12-hour clock and the 24-hour clock

Remember

24-hour clock			12-hour clock
00:00	(midnight)	is	12.00 am
07:30		is	7.30 am
11:59		is	11.59 am
12:00	(midday)	is	12.00 pm
12:59		is	12.59 pm
13:00		is	1.00 pm
16:05		is	4.05 pm
23:59		is	11.59 pm

TOP TIP

Just a minute!
A minute is quite a long time.
It is long enough to draw, name
and mark the equal sides and
angles of all of the quadrilaterals.
It is long enough to do a 7 × 7
jumbled multiplication square.
It is long enough to list the
prime numbers below a
hundred. Don't waste a
minute!

- After 12.59 pm, to change from 12-hour clock times to 24-hour clock times, we simply add 12 It is necessary to take care around lunchtime!

- It is important to be able to understand **timetables** such as bus or train timetables.

- It is also useful to understand different times around the world.

What time?

- Study a bus or train timetable. Ask, and answer, questions such as 'How long will it take to travel from X to Y?'

- Study a TV guide. Ask, and answer, questions such as 'How long is that film?'

- Study times around the world.

Measurement of speed

AIM HIGH

- Speed is the distance travelled in one unit of time.

Units include

- **metric** units: metres per second (m/s), kilometres per hour (km/h)

    Think of:

    1 km/h   →   0.28 m/s   a very fast mouse

- **Imperial** units: miles per hour (miles/h or mph)

    Think of:

    5 mph   →   fast walking speed

Useful conversions to remember

30 mph	→	48 km/h
60 mph	→	96 km/h

Reading scales

- Many measuring instruments have linear scales like those below.

0 ————————————————————————— 10

0 ———————————— 0.5 ———————————— 1

0 ————————————————————————— 5

- Notice how the intervals can vary. It is very important to find out what each little division represents.

- Some instruments have scales which are circular, but they are read in the same way.

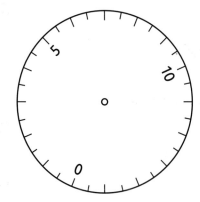

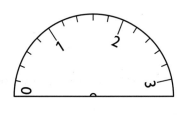

Metric conversion

Prepare your own table of Imperial/metric conversions, such as

1 mile   →   1609 m

AIM HIGH

Questions

The answers are at the back of the book.

5.4 (a) Write as 24-hour clock times:

     (i)   1.09 pm   (1)

     (ii) 6.45 am   (1)

   (b) Write as am/pm times:

     (i)   18:36   (1)

     (ii) 20:15   (1)

5.5 What are the readings on these scales?

   (i)   (1)

   (ii)   (1)

   (iii)   (2)

   (iv)   (2)

Multiple choice questions

In these questions you should write the letter of the correct answer.

5.6 The mass of a hockey ball is approximately   (1)

   A: **16 g**   B: **26 g**   C: **160 g**   D: **260 g**   E: **1.6 kg**

5.7 An ordinary mug (for drinking tea etc) has a capacity of about   (1)

   A: **25 ml**   B: **50 ml**   C: **100 ml**   D: **150 ml**   E: **200 ml**

5.8 A sheet of A4 paper has an area of about   (1)

   A: **60 cm²**   B: **300 cm²**   C: **600 cm²**   D: **1000 cm²**   E: **6000 cm²**

5.2 SHAPE

Plane shapes

Plane (flat) shapes are **two-dimensional** shapes.

They have sides, vertices (corners) and angles.

They may have

- diagonals – lines drawn across the shape (not necessarily through the mid-point) from one vertex to another
- one or more lines of symmetry
- rotational symmetry about the mid-point.

Triangles

A **triangle** is a **plane shape**.

A triangle has 3 sides, 3 vertices and 3 angles.

Types of triangle are:

- **equilateral**   3 equal sides and 3 equal angles
- **isosceles**   2 equal sides and 2 equal angles
- **right-angled** one 90° angle
- **scalene**   no equal sides and no equal angles.

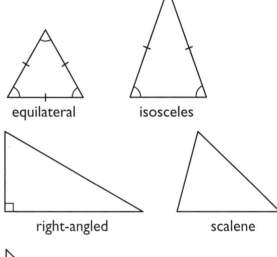

equilateral   isosceles

right-angled   scalene

- It is possible for a triangle to be both isosceles and right-angled.

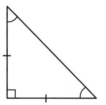

Quadrilaterals

Quadrilaterals have 4 sides, 4 vertices and 4 angles.

Types of quadrilaterals are:

- **square**   all sides equal; all angles equal (90°); opposite sides parallel; diagonals equal

- **rectangle**   opposite sides equal and parallel; all angles equal (90°); diagonals equal

- **rhombus**   all sides equal; opposite angles equal; opposite sides parallel; diagonals *not* equal but cross at 90°

- **parallelogram** opposite sides equal and parallel; opposite angles equal; diagonals *not* equal

- **kite**   two pairs of adjacent equal sides; one pair of opposite equal angles; diagonals *not* equal but cross at 90°

- **trapezium**   one pair of opposite parallel sides; diagonals *not* equal except in isosceles trapezium (see below).

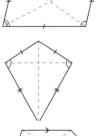

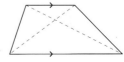

You will probably meet two special quadrilaterals:

- **delta (arrowhead) kite**   one angle is reflex (more than 180°)

- **isosceles trapezium**   the two non-parallel sides equal; two pairs of adjacent angles equal; diagonals equal.

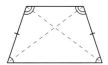

Making quadrilaterals

Study quadrilaterals made by making straight cuts across folded paper.

See if you can make

- a square

- a rhombus

- a kite.

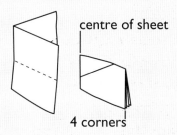

First, fold a sheet of paper exactly in two.
Then make a second fold which can be either

- at right-angles to the first fold, or

- at an acute angle to the first fold.

Polygons

A **polygon** has many sides. Types of polygon are

- **pentagon**   5 sides

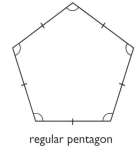

regular pentagon

pentagon

- **hexagon**   6 sides

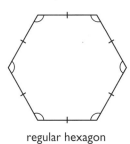

regular hexagon

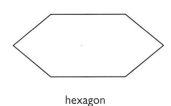

hexagon

- **heptagon**   7 sides
- **octagon**   8 sides
- **nonagon**   9 sides
- **decagon**   10 sides

A regular polygon has all sides and angles equal.

Symmetry

Here are examples of plane shapes which have

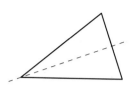 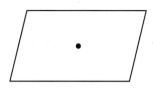 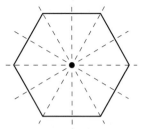 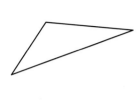

reflection symmetry   rotation symmetry   both reflection and   no symmetry
rotation symmetry

Reflection symmetry

- All of the lines of reflection symmetry are drawn on the shapes below as dotted lines.

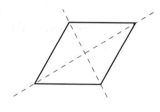 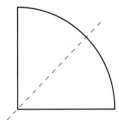 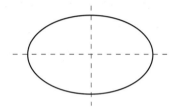 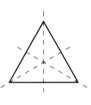

- A line of reflection can be considered as a mirror line.
  You could place a mirror on the line of symmetry and see the hidden half of the shape in the mirror.

- An equilateral triangle has 3 lines of symmetry.

- A square has 4 lines of symmetry.

- The decorated square below has two lines of symmetry!

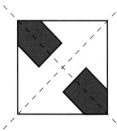

You will notice that the two lines of symmetry are at right angles.

> **TOP TIP**
> When you look in a mirror, you do not see yourself as others see you! See if you can find out why this is.

- In the drawing on the right, a design has been reflected in the dotted line to form a new shape. The dotted line is a line of symmetry of the new shape.

- The two halves of a shape on either side of the line of symmetry are the same shape and size, but they are mirror images of each other. The two halves are **congruent**.

line of symmetry

Rotational symmetry

- A shape has rotational symmetry about its mid-point if it can be rotated to fit onto itself in more than one way. The number of ways is called the **order of rotational symmetry**.

- A square has rotational symmetry of order 4

- A regular pentagon has rotational symmetry of order 5

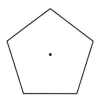

- This decorated square has rotational symmetry of order 4 but it has no lines of symmetry.

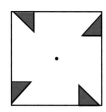

Cut-outs with lines of symmetry

Make a display of cut-outs with different numbers of lines of symmetry. Three examples are shown below. Can you make a cut-out with three lines of symmetry?

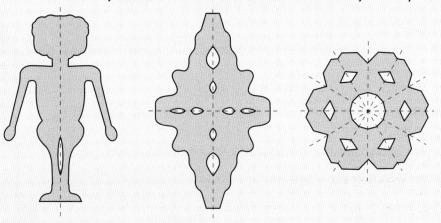

Symmetry challenge

The square below has area 25 cm², 4 lines of symmetry and rotational symmetry of order 4

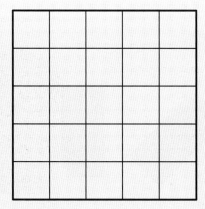

On centimetre squared paper, draw four shapes, W, X, Y and Z, *all with area 25 cm²*, and with the following extra features:

- Shape W   no symmetry at all
- Shape X   two lines of symmetry and rotation symmetry order 2
- Shape Y   no reflection symmetry but rotation symmetry order 2
- Shape Z   no reflection symmetry but rotation symmetry order 4

Hint: start with a 5 cm square each time and modify it.

Questions

The answers are at the back of the book.

5.9 Three quadrilaterals are drawn below.

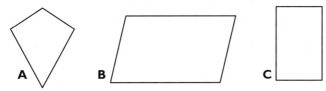

  (i)   Name the shapes.   (3)

  (ii) Copy the shapes. Draw all lines of symmetry on the shapes.   (3)

  (iii) Describe the rotational symmetry of the shapes.   (2)

5.10 Amy has drawn a triangle, accurately, on a piece of paper and hidden it.

Ben has asked two questions which are listed below, in order, together with Amy's answers.

  Question 1   'Are any angles the same?'   Answer: 'Yes'

  Question 2   'Is one angle a right angle?'   Answer: 'Yes'

  (i)   Sketch Amy's triangle.   (2)

  (ii) If Amy's answer to question 2 had been 'No', suggest a suitable third question for Ben to ask.   (2)

Congruence

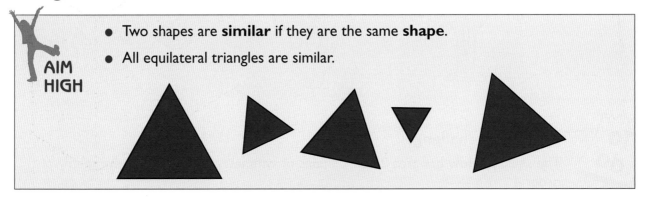

- Two shapes are **similar** if they are the same **shape**.
- All equilateral triangles are similar.

AIM HIGH

- Two shapes are **congruent** if they are **identical** in **shape** and **size**.

- It does not matter if one needs to be reflected or rotated.

- The shapes below are all congruent.

Solid shapes

Solid shapes are **three-dimensional** shapes. They have faces, edges and vertices (corners).

They may have

- one or more planes of symmetry

- axes of rotational symmetry.

Solid shapes include:

- **cube**   6 square faces; 8 vertices; 12 edges
- **cuboid**   6 rectangular faces; 8 vertices; 12 edges
- **tetrahedron**   4 equilateral triangular faces; 4 vertices; 6 edges
- **square pyramid**   1 square face; 4 isosceles triangular faces; 5 vertices; 8 edges
- **triangular prism**   2 equilateral triangular end faces, 3 rectangular faces, 6 vertices, 9 edges

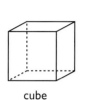 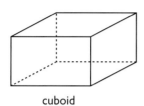 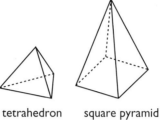 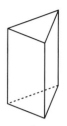

      cube   cuboid   tetrahedron   square pyramid   triangular prism

Drawing solids

- We can draw a picture of a solid shape on an **isometric** grid.
- The diagram shows a picture of a cuboid measuring 5 cm × 2 cm × 4 cm.

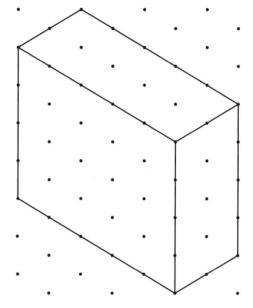

AIM HIGH

The same idea can be used for irregular solids such as models made from interlocking centimetre cubes.

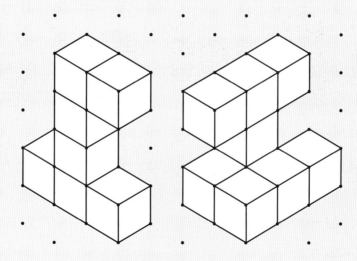

Nets

A **net** of a solid shape

- shows all the faces of the shape, with appropriate faces joined together
- can be folded up to make the shape.

The diagram below shows examples of nets for the solid shapes listed on page 115.

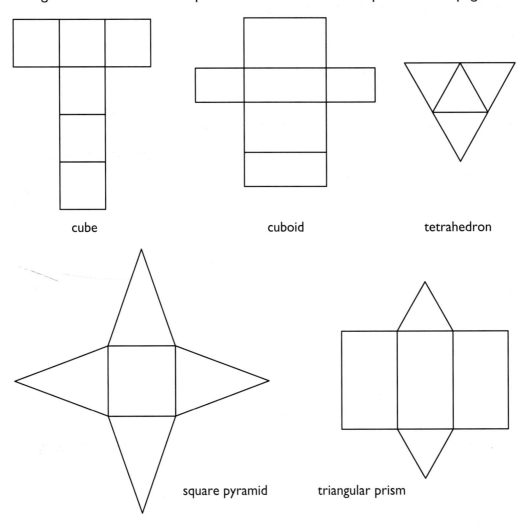

cube   cuboid   tetrahedron

square pyramid   triangular prism

- Look carefully at each net and see how it can fold up to make the solid shape.
- Try to work out which sides join together to make each edge of the solid.
- It is possible to draw several different nets for a solid shape.
- Here are three of the possible 11 nets for a cube.

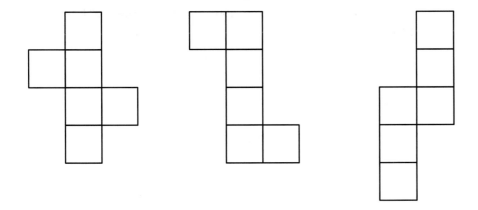

Models of solids

Make models of the five solids using enlarged copies of the nets shown on page 116.

Using suitable thin card, such as an empty cereal packet

- draw the net on the plain side of the card

- carefully 'score' along the lines joining faces

- cut out the net

- fold along the lines joining the faces

- fold up the faces to make the solid

- use tape or suitable glue to fix the edges of the solid.

Attractive solid shapes can be made by folding so that the printed side of the cereal packet forms the outside of the shape.

Study your shapes by

- counting the numbers of faces, vertices and edges

- counting the number of faces which meet at a vertex

- counting the number of edges which meet at a vertex

- looking at the symmetry.

Solid shapes from centimetre cubes

You will need a supply of centimetre cubes.

To make a model, you should carefully stick the cubes together, face to face, using a suitable adhesive.

Interlocking centimetre cubes avoid the need for adhesive and can be re-used.

Activity 1
Make as many different solids as you can from 3 cubes, then progress to 4 cubes and finally to 5 cubes.

Activity 2
On an isometric dotted grid, draw a representation of a solid and then make a model from centimetre cubes.

Look at your model from different viewpoints and draw representations of two different views of the same solid.

Shapes dominoes

Make a set of shapes dominoes, or use a copy of the set in Appendix 3, page 159, and make a spinner like the one shown below.

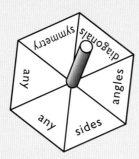

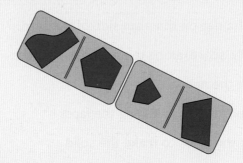

You could make up your own rules, but try these two games first.

Game 1 rules

- Share out the dominoes between the players, with any remaining dominoes put to one side.

- Roll a die to decide who starts.

- Before each player puts down a domino, spin the spinner to decide if the 'match' must be concerned with facts about

  - o sides   such as 'sides all equal' or 'opposite sides parallel'

  - o angles   such as 'opposite angles equal'

  - o diagonals   such as 'diagonals cross at 90°'

  - o symmetry   such as 'one line of symmetry' or 'rotational symmetry order 2'.

- The other players act as judges to ensure fair play!

- If a player cannot make a match, then he/she takes a spare domino if possible.

- The first player with no dominoes left is the winner.

Game 2 rules

- Share out the dominoes between the players, with any remaining dominoes put to one side.

- Roll a die to decide who starts.

- A player should strive to get the largest number of matches (maximum 1 match each for sides, angles, diagonals and symmetry) when each domino is put down.

EXAMPLE:

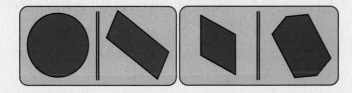

Here the player could claim 4 points by declaring '4 sides; opposite angles equal; diagonals not equal; rotation symmetry order 2'.

- The other players act as judges to ensure fair play.

- When all of the dominoes have been played, the player with most points is the winner.

Questions

The answers are at the back of the book.

5.11 Study the shapes drawn on the grid below.

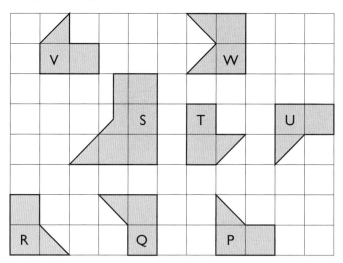

(i) Which shape is *similar* to shape P?	(1)
(ii) Which shapes are *congruent* to shape P?	(3)

5.12 The drawing shows a cuboid made from centimetre squared paper.

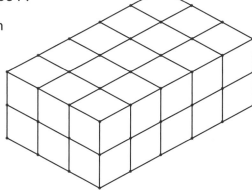

(i) On a sheet of centimetre squared paper, draw an accurate net for the cuboid.	(3)
(ii) What is the volume of the cuboid?	(2)
(iii) What area of paper is needed to make the cuboid?	(3)

Multiple choice questions

In these questions you should write the letter of the correct answer.

5.13 How many of the quadrilaterals below have diagonals of equal length? (1)

square	kite	parallelogram
rectangle	rhombus	isosceles trapezium

A: 1   B: 2   C: 3   D: 4   E: 5

5.14 Which of the shapes below has *no* lines of symmetry? (1)

A: **square**   B: **rhombus**   C: **kite**

D: **parallelogram**   E: **isosceles trapezium**

5.15 How many of the shapes below have rotational symmetry? (1)

square	rhombus	isosceles triangle
kite	rectangle	parallelogram
equilateral triangle	scalene triangle	

A: 4   B: 5   C: 6   D: 7   E: 8

5.3 SPACE

Angles

What is an angle?

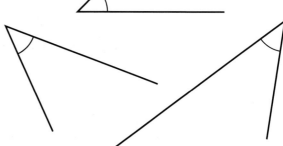

- An **angle** is the size of the turn when two lines, joined at one end, are 'hinged open'.

- The length of the lines does not matter!

- All of these angles are half a right angle (45°).

- An angle can be any size from 0° (no turn) to 360° (one complete turn).

Types of angle

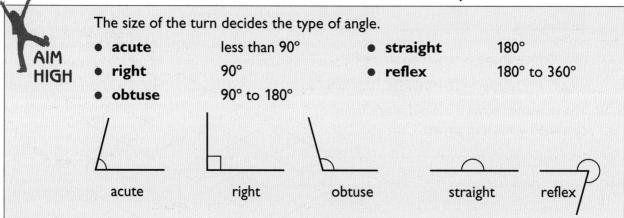

The size of the turn decides the type of angle.

- **acute**   less than 90°   • **straight**   180°
- **right**   90°   • **reflex**   180° to 360°
- **obtuse**   90° to 180°

AIM HIGH

acute   right   obtuse   straight   reflex

Measuring angles

Angles can be measured using a **geoliner** or **protractor**.

- It is important to know how to position your own instrument.

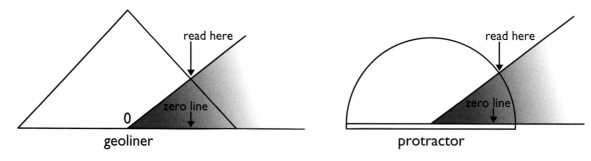

read here   read here

zero line   zero line

0

geoliner   protractor

○ Place the 'centre' mark of the instrument on the 'corner' of the angle.

○ Make sure that a zero line is placed on one 'arm' of the angle.

○ Count round from zero until you reach the second arm of the angle.

○ Read off the angle on the scale.

○ Check to see if the number of degrees is appropriate – for example, less than 90° if the angle is acute.

- For a reflex angle, remember that you will need to add 180° unless you have a circular, 360° protractor.

Estimating angles

Sometimes you may be asked to estimate an angle.

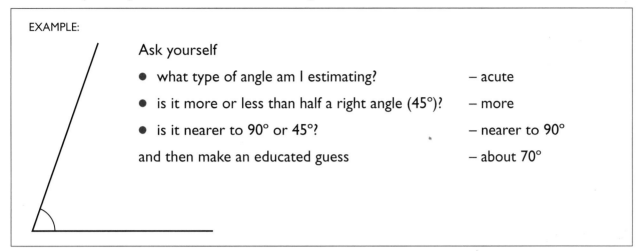

EXAMPLE:

Ask yourself

- what type of angle am I estimating?   – acute
- is it more or less than half a right angle (45°)?   – more
- is it nearer to 90° or 45°?   – nearer to 90°

and then make an educated guess   – about 70°

Drawing angles

Angles can be drawn using a geoliner or protractor and ruler.

- As with measuring angles, it is important to know how to position your own instrument.
  - Place the 'centre' mark of the instrument on the 'corner' of the angle.
  - Make sure that a zero line is placed on the 'arm' of the angle.
  - Count round from zero until you reach the required angle.
  - Put a neat pencil mark beside the angle on the scale of the instrument.
  - Check to see that you have the right type of angle – for example, obtuse if the angle to be drawn is between 90° and 180°.
- For a reflex angle, remember that you will need to add 180° unless you have a circular, 360° protractor.

TOP TIP

Use a sharp pencil when drawing angles.

Useful angle facts

There are several useful angle facts in addition to those already described in section 5.2 (pages 100–111).

Angles which are equal

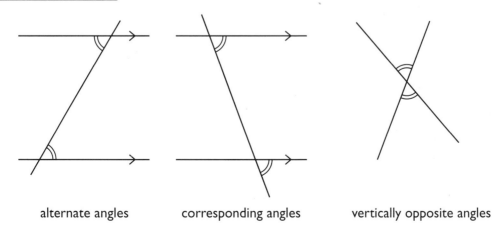

alternate angles   corresponding angles   vertically opposite angles

Angles which add up to 180°

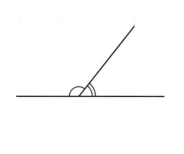

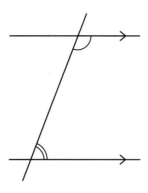

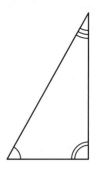

angles on a straight line   supplementary angles   angles in a triangle

Angles which add up to 360°

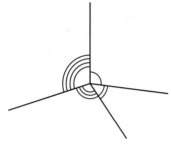

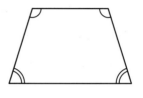

angles at a point   angles in a quadrilateral

To do

Angles card game

Make a set of angles cards. The angles should

- cover a complete range from 10° to 350° going up in 10° steps

- have arms of different lengths

- be shaded, as in the examples shown.

Rules

- Shuffle the cards and deal them out, with any remaining cards left to one side and hidden.

- Roll a die to decide who goes first.

- The first player can put down any card.

- The players then take it in turns to play a larger angle card.

- If a player 'can't go' then a spare card is taken if available.

- When no-one can play a larger angle card, then the rule switches to playing a smaller angle card.

- The first player to be left with no cards is the winner.

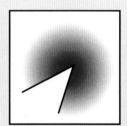

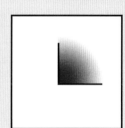

You can put in additional rules such as: a player must say what **type** of angle is being played or **estimate** the angle being played.

Angle sum: triangle

You will need sheets of thin card (such as from a cereal packet), or stiff paper, and scissors.

- Draw a large triangle and cut it out carefully.
- Tear off all three corners and fit the corners together along a straight edge. What do you notice?
- Repeat for a different triangle.

Angle sum: quadrilateral

You will need sheets of thin card (such as from a cereal packet), or stiff paper, and scissors.

- Draw a large parallelogram and cut it out carefully.
- Tear off all four corners and fit the corners together. What do you notice?
- Repeat for other quadrilaterals including trapezium, kite and delta kite.

Questions

The answers are at the back of the book.

5.16 For each of the angles below, *without measuring*, write down

- the type of angle (acute etc)
- an estimate of the angle.

(2 marks for each angle)

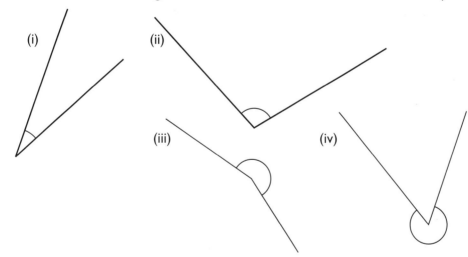

5.17 (a) (i) Measure, to the nearest degree, each
angle of triangle *ABC*.   (3)

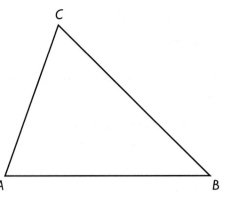

(ii) Write down the sum of the angles of triangle *ABC*.   (1)

(b) Triangle *DEF* is drawn below.

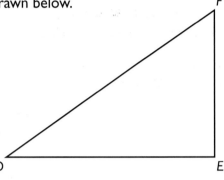

(i) What type of angle is
(a) angle *DEF*   (1)
(b) angle *DFE*?   (1)

(ii) What name is given to this type of triangle?   (1)

5.18 Find the angles represented by the six letters in the diagrams below by working them out.
Do not measure them.

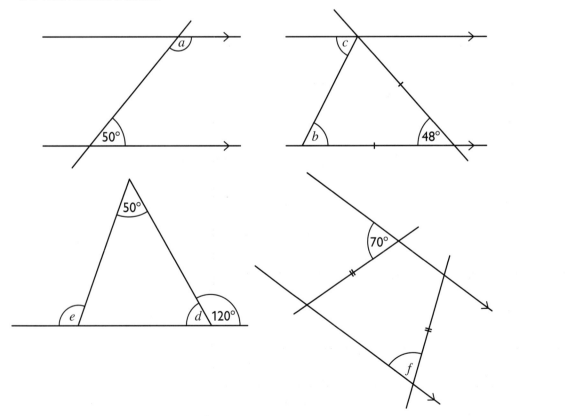

(6)

The eight-point compass

Compass points

- The four main points of the compass, in order clockwise, are north (N), east (E), south (S) and west (W).

- It is easy to remember the directions of these. North and south present no problem and the only confusion for some people lies with west and east. To help you remember that W is on the left and E is on the right:

  - W – E forms the word 'WE'

  - When people talk about 'the west' they usually refer to America and when they talk about 'the east' they usually refer to Japan, China and so on.

  - You might prefer to remember the mnemonic '**N**aughty **E**lephants **S**quirt **W**ater *round the clock*'. The '*round the clock*' is very important since the **NESW** must be clockwise!

- Between the four main compass directions are four more: north-east (NE), south-east (SE), south-west (SW) and north-west (NW).

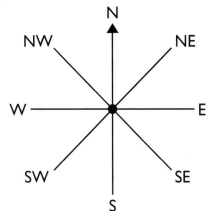

- Note that in these four

  - there are two letters

  - N or S is always placed first.

- In the scale drawing below

  - Robin is standing north of Shannon

  - Shannon is standing west of Trevor

  - Una is standing south-west of Shannon

  - Shannon is north-east of Una.

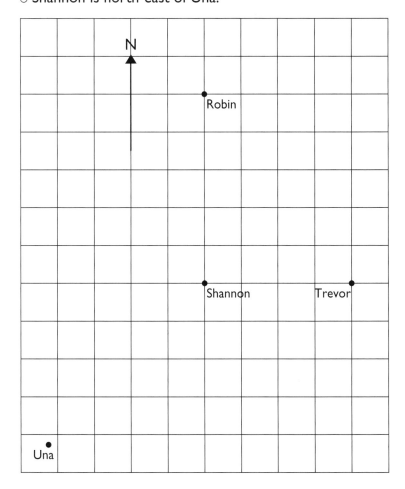

Bearings

AIM HIGH

The eight points of the compass are very useful but sometimes we want to describe a direction which lies somewhere in between and we need to do this very accurately.

Each of the eight compass directions is given a **bearing**.

N	000°
NE	045°
E	090°
SE	135°
S	180°
SW	225°
W	270°
NW	315°

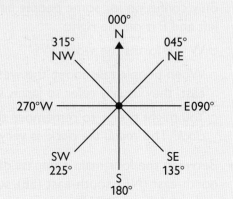

- Remember that bearings are always given
  ○ clockwise from north
  ○ as three figures.

Scale drawings

AIM HIGH

- Have another look at the scale drawing on page 125.

- In the drawing, 1 cm represents 1 m.

- You will see that
  ○ Robin is standing 5 m north of Shannon
  ○ Shannon is standing 4 m west of Trevor
  ○ Una is standing 6 m south-west of Shannon
  ○ Shannon is 6 m north-east of Una.

- We can write the scale as:
  ○ 1 cm represents 1 m, or
  ○ 1 : 100   (since 1 cm represents 100 cm)
  ○ or we can show it as a small diagram.

1 m

TOP TIP

Remember 'WE' can help with learning the points of the compass.

To do

Positions using paces and compass directions

Ideally you should do this outside on a lawn or playing field.

You will need:

- a few friends
- a suitable compass
- eight pieces of ribbon or string (each about 2 m long)
- nine thin metal tent pegs or 6 inch nails
- a sheet of A4 centimetre squared paper, pencil and ruler.

Decide on a suitable starting point in the middle of a space.

Peg the pieces of ribbon, in straight lines, in the eight compass directions from this point. Remind everyone that a **pace** is a *normal* walking stride. Now you are ready to start. ▶

Instructions

- Each person, in turn, should be asked to walk
  - a number of paces that you decide
  - in one of the eight compass directions that you decide

  and then sit down.

- The recorder should, on the sheet of A4 paper,
  - keep a note of the number of paces and directions walked
  - prepare a scale drawing (1 cm to represent 2 paces might be appropriate) showing the sitting positions of everyone.

From this stage, someone could walk from one person to another in a straight line, counting the number of paces. This number of paces could be compared with the corresponding measurement on the scale drawing.

Transformations

- There are three **transformations** which can move a shape without changing its shape or size. The original shape and its **image** are **congruent**.

Reflection

- A shape can be **reflected** in a **line** to form a mirror image of the shape.

mirror line

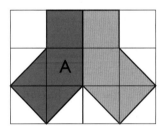

Rotation

- A shape can be **rotated** through an **angle** (usually 90° or 180°) about a **point**.

TOP TIP

The rotation can be either clockwise or anticlockwise.

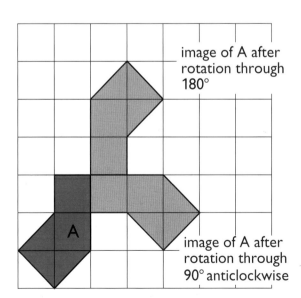

image of A after rotation through 180°

image of A after rotation through 90° anticlockwise

Translation

- A shape can be **translated** a number of units **right** (or **left**) and a number of units **up** (or **down**) as shown in the diagram.

- We could follow one translation by another.

EXAMPLE: 5 units right and 6 units up followed by 3 units left and 8 units down would be equivalent to 2 units right and 2 units down.

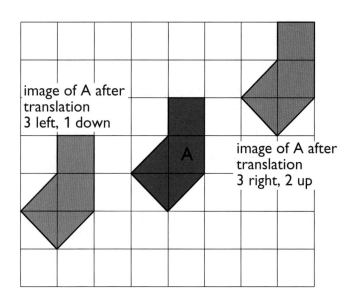

image of A after translation 3 left, 1 down

image of A after translation 3 right, 2 up

AIM HIGH

If positive and negative numbers are used instead of the words left, right, up and down, then a negative number indicates left or down.

Transformations on a grid

- On the grid below, triangle **A** has been
  - reflected in **line _m_** to form triangle **B**
  - reflected in **line _n_** to form triangle **C**
  - rotated through **180°** about point **X** to form triangle **D**
  - rotated through **90° anticlockwise** about point **Y** to form triangle **E**
  - translated **5 units right** and **6 units up** to form triangle **F**.

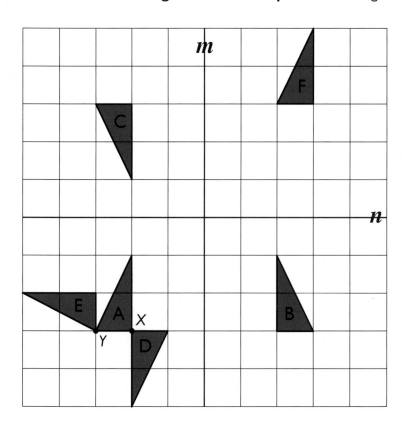

Questions

The answers are at the back of the book.

5.19 The scale drawing below shows five pupils standing on a patio made with 50 cm square concrete slabs.

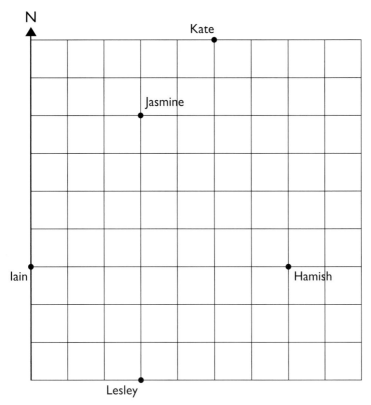

Write down the compass direction of

(i)   Hamish from Iain   (2)

(ii) Jasmine from Hamish   (2)

(iii) Kate from Jasmine   (2)

(iv) Iain from Lesley   (2)

(v)   Jasmine from Lesley.   (2)

5.20 Copy the diagram and reflect the shape in line *m*.   (3)

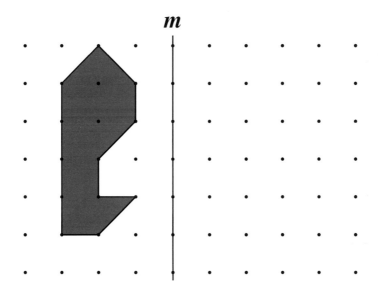

5.21 On a copy of the grid below,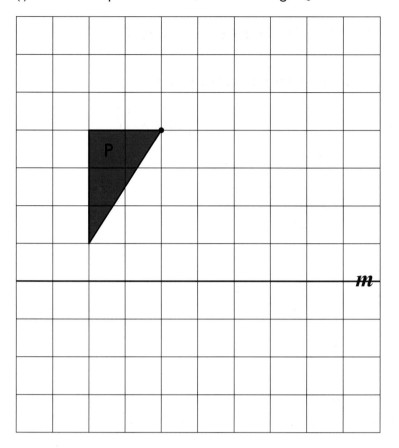

    (i)   reflect shape **P** in line *m*; label the image **Q**   (2)

    (ii)   rotate shape **P** through 90° anti-clockwise about the dot; label the image **R**   (2)

    (iii) translate shape **P** 4 units right and 3 units up; label the image **S**.   (2)

Triangle construction

We can construct a triangle if we know

1 the lengths of all three sides

AIM HIGH

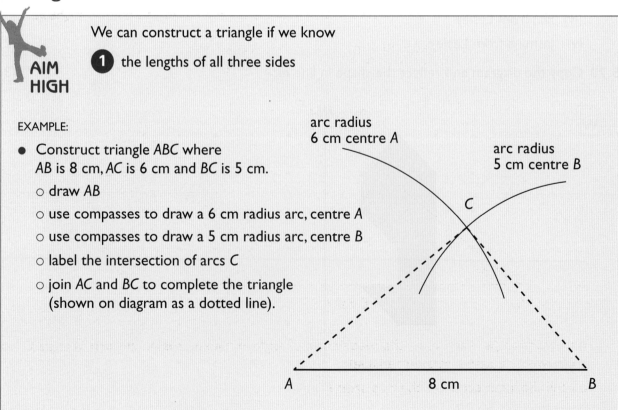

EXAMPLE:

- Construct triangle *ABC* where
  AB is 8 cm, *AC* is 6 cm and *BC* is 5 cm.

  ○ draw *AB*

  ○ use compasses to draw a 6 cm radius arc, centre *A*

  ○ use compasses to draw a 5 cm radius arc, centre *B*

  ○ label the intersection of arcs *C*

  ○ join *AC* and *BC* to complete the triangle
    (shown on diagram as a dotted line).

2 the lengths of two sides and the angle between them

EXAMPLE:

● Construct triangle *DEF* where *DE* is 6 cm, *DF* is 6 cm and angle *D* is 40°.

  ○ draw *DE*

  ○ use a geoliner or protractor to draw the second arm of angle *D*

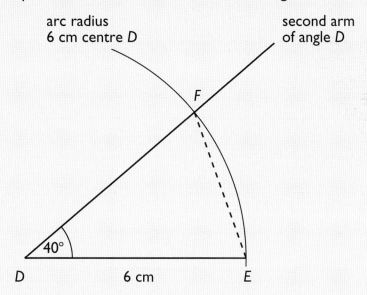

arc radius
6 cm centre *D*

second arm
of angle *D*

F

40°

D   6 cm   *E*

  ○ draw *DF* (measure along second arm of angle or draw arc)

  ○ join *EF* to complete the triangle (shown on diagram as a dotted line).

3 two angles and the length of the side between them.

EXAMPLE:

● Construct triangle *GHI* where *GH* is 8 cm, angle *G* is 40° and angle *H* is 50°

  ○ draw *GH*

  ○ measure angle *G* and draw the second arm of angle *G* longer than you think it might be

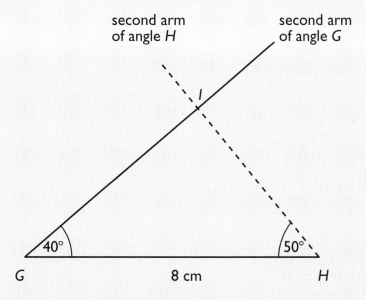

second arm
of angle *H*

second arm
of angle *G*

I

40°   50°

G   8 cm   *H*

  ○ measure angle *H* and draw the second arm of angle *H* until it crosses the arm of angle *G* (shown on diagram as a dotted line)

  ○ label the intersection of the two arms *I*.

Triangles

On a copy of the four-quadrant co-ordinate grid below:

- Plot the points with co-ordinates (1, 1), (3, 1) and (3, 3).

- Join the points to form triangle A.

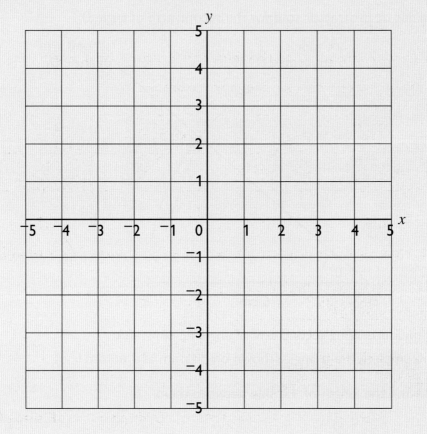

- Rotate triangle A through 180° about the origin (0, 0) and label the new triangle B.

- Rotate triangle A though 90° clockwise about the origin and label the new triangle C.

- Reflect triangle A in the x-axis (the line $y = 0$) and label the new triangle D.

- Translate triangle A 4 units to the left and 6 units down and label the new triangle E.

On a new copy of the grid:

- Draw a triangle of your own and label it P.

- Make up some instructions of your own to rotate, reflect and translate triangle P.

Questions

The answers are at the back of the book.

5.22 (i) Construct triangle *ABC* where *AB* is 7 cm, *BC* is 6 cm and *AC* is 5 cm. (3)

(ii) Measure, to the nearest degree, angle *ACB*. (1)

Multiple choice questions

In these questions you should write the letter of the correct answer.

5.23 How many of the shapes below are congruent to shape **P**? (1)

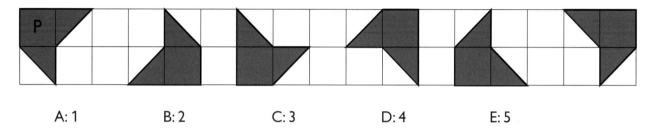

A: 1   B: 2   C: 3   D: 4   E: 5

5.24 On the grid below, which shape could *not* be mapped onto shape **J** by rotation? (1)

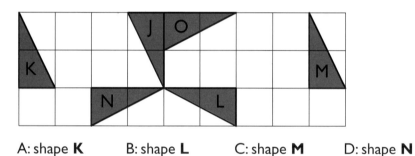

A: shape **K**   B: shape **L**   C: shape **M**   D: shape **N**   E: shape **O**

The next three questions concern the quadrilateral *PQRS* shown below.

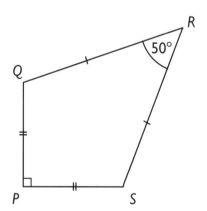

5.25 What name is given to this quadrilateral? (1)

A: **square**   B: **trapezium**   C: **rectangle**   D: **rhombus**   E: **kite**

5.26 What type of angle is angle *PQR*? (1)

A: **acute**   B: **right**   C: **obtuse**   D: **straight**   E: **reflex**

5.27 If angle *SPQ* is a right-angle and angle *SRQ* is 50°, what is the size of angle *PQR*? (1)

A: **100°**   B: **105°**   C: **110°**   D: **125°**   E: **230°**

`6 HANDLING DATA

Can you imagine a world without data? Data is everywhere − lists, tables including timetables, charts, graphs, spreadsheets, averages and so on. Statistics can sometimes be made to look better than they are to mislead people, so it is important to gain a good understanding. Probability features in many games and, of course, the National Lottery!

6.1 DATA HANDLING

Raw data

Types of data

- **Discrete data** is usually associated with counting, using integers.

> EXAMPLE: the numbers of cars of different colours passing under a motorway bridge. Intermediate points have no meaning. For example 3.5 cars is not possible.

- **Continuous data** is usually associated with measurement.

> EXAMPLE 1: masses of people − there are countless small increases from 40 kg to 50 kg.
>
> EXAMPLE 2: temperatures − the temperature doesn't 'jump' from 9 °C to 10 °C.

Collecting and recording raw data

Data can be collected and recorded in a variety of ways.

- **List**

> EXAMPLE: Recording the sex of pupils as they stand in line.
>
> **Boy/Girl**
>
> boy
> girl
> girl
> boy
> boy
> girl
> boy
> girl
> girl
> girl
> girl
> girl

- **Table**

> EXAMPLE: Recording the types of pet owned in a dog/cat survey.
>
> | Name | Dog | Cat |
> |------|-----|-----|
> | Andy | ✓ | |
> | Bea | ✓ | ✓ |
> | Celia | | ✓ |
> | David | ✓ | |
> | Eddie | | ✓ |
> | Fran | ✓ | ✓ |
> | George | | |
> | Helen | ✓ | |
> | Irene | | ✓ |
> | June | ✓ | |
> | Kath | ✓ | ✓ |
> | Lara | ✓ | ✓ |

- **Tally and frequency table**

In a **tally**, the tally marks / are recorded in blocks of 5 like this:

/	//	///	////	#####	##### /
1	2	3	4	5	6

EXAMPLE: Recording the scores obtained with a pentagonal spinner.

Score	Tally					Frequency
1	#####	#####	#####	#####	//	22
2	#####	#####	#####	#####		20
3	#####	#####	#####	///		18
4	#####	#####	#####	#####	///	23
5	#####	#####	#####	//		17
					Total	**100**

- A **frequency table** is often produced with a tally, as in the example above.

- The frequency for each score is the sum of the tallies.

Traffic survey

Carry out a simple traffic survey. You could record, as a tally,

- the numbers of different coloured cars passing your house

- the numbers of people in each car.

When you have recorded the data, represent it by a suitable diagram (such as a pictogram, block graph or bar chart) and comment on the results.

Sorting raw data

Raw data can be **sorted** (**grouped**)

- using a **flow chart**

EXAMPLE: Here we have sorted the children with dogs and/or cats (see the table on page 134).

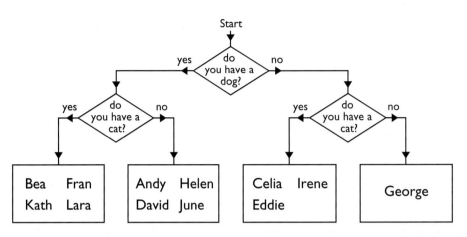

- using a **key**

EXAMPLE: Keys are used to identify organisms in natural history.

We will identify a quadrilateral using a similar key, as an example.

1. Does it have reflection symmetry?
   Yes: go to 3
   No: go to 2

2. Does it have rotation symmetry?
   Yes: it is a **parallelogram**
   No: it is a non-isosceles **trapezium**

3. Are all sides equal?
   Yes: go to 4
   No: go to 5

4. Are all angles equal?
   Yes: it is a **square**
   No: it is a **rhombus**

5. Are all angles right angles?
   Yes: it is a **rectangle**
   No: go to 6

6. Is one pair of sides parallel?
   Yes: it is an **isosceles trapezium**
   No: it is a **kite**

What is it called?

Use the key above to identify the following quadrilaterals:

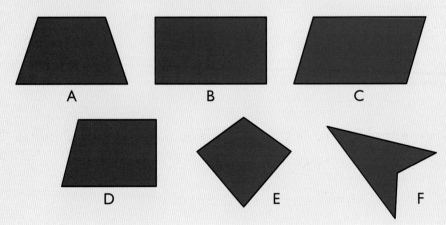

Representing data

You can represent the data recorded in the examples on pages 134–135 in several ways.

Carroll diagram

EXAMPLE: Dogs and cats survey

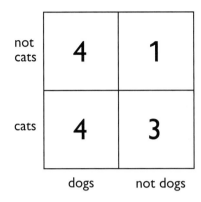

	dogs	not dogs
not cats	Andy David Helen June	George
cats	Bea Fran Kath Lara	Celia Irene Eddie

	dogs	not dogs
not cats	4	1
cats	4	3

- In the diagram on the left, we have put the names of the children in the appropriate regions.
- In the diagram on the right, we have simply put in the numbers of children.
- You can see at a glance that a total of 8 children own dogs and 4 children own both dogs and cats.

Venn diagram

EXAMPLE: Dogs and cats survey

- The diagram represents the same data as the right-hand Carroll diagram above.
- Notice how the regions of the two types of diagram correspond.

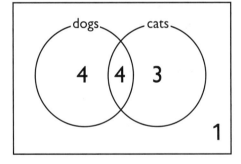

Friends survey

Decide on two things to investigate about your friends such as

- left-handed
- wears glasses

or

- has one or more brothers
- has one or more sisters.

Collect and record the data in a table like the one for dogs and cats on page 134.

Represent the data as a Carroll diagram and as a Venn diagram.

Comment on your results.

Pictogram

EXAMPLE: Boys and girls in line

- In this pictogram one symbol represents one child, as stated in the **key**.

Key: one symbol 😊 represents 1 child

- Sometimes a symbol can represent more than one thing. For example, if the key indicates that one symbol represents 2 people then 1 person could be represented by 😊 half a symbol.

- A pictogram *must* have a key.

Block graph

EXAMPLE:

- This block graph represents the same data as the pictogram above.

- Here one block represents one child.

- As with a pictogram it is important to have a key to say what each block represents.

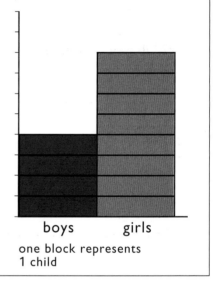

one block represents 1 child

Bar chart

EXAMPLE:

- This bar chart also represents the data about boys and girls.

- As with the pictogram and block graph, we can compare the number of boys to the number of girls.

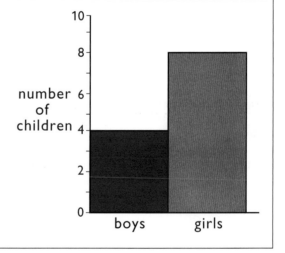

Fraction diagram

EXAMPLE:

- The fraction diagram (see also Chapter 1 page 34) allows us to see the proportion of boys in the group of children.

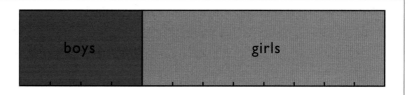

Pie chart

EXAMPLE:

- This pie chart represents the same (boy/girl) data.

- 8 of the 12 children are girls.

- This can be considered as 2 out of every 3, or $\frac{2}{3}$ of the children, so $\frac{2}{3}$ of the 'pie' is labelled 'girls'.

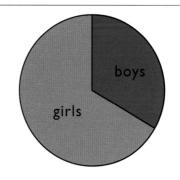

Bar line graph

EXAMPLE:

- The lengths of the bar lines show the frequencies of the various scores when spinning the pentagonal spinner (see page 135).

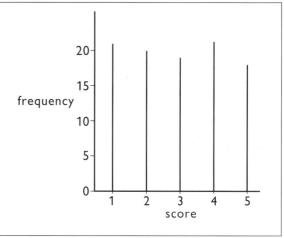

Frequency diagram

EXAMPLE:

- This frequency diagram represents the same data as the bar line graph above.

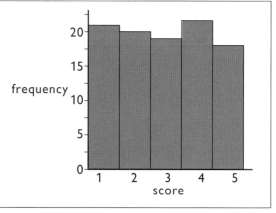

Are any numbers lucky?

Make a spinner. You might like to be imaginative and make an unusual one like this heptagonal spinner.

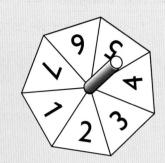

Number it 1, 2, …, 7

Spin the spinner a suitable number of times (70 might be a good number for this spinner) and record the results in a tally.

Represent your results as a bar line graph or frequency diagram.

Questions

The answers are at the back of the book.

6.1 Here are ten integers:

| 12 | 13 | 21 | 28 | 54 | 42 | 6 | 49 | 14 | 36 |

(i) On a copy of this Carroll diagram, write each of the above numbers in the correct region. (5)

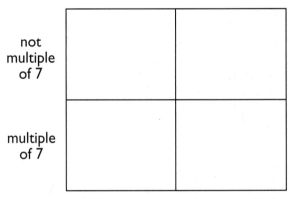

(ii) On a copy of this Venn diagram, write each number in the correct region. (5)

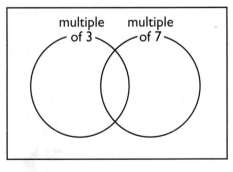

(iii) For the ten integers above, what is the

    (a) range (1)

    (b) median (2)

    (c) mean? (2)

(Range, median and mean are covered on page 142.)

6.2 The pictogram below shows the money raised for charity by six friends.

Key: ⬤ represents **£2**

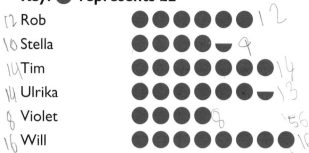

12 Rob ⬤⬤⬤⬤⬤⬤ 12
10 Stella ⬤⬤⬤⬤◗ 9
14 Tim ⬤⬤⬤⬤⬤⬤⬤ 14
14 Ulrika ⬤⬤⬤⬤⬤⬤◗ 13
8 Violet ⬤⬤⬤⬤ 8
16 Will ⬤⬤⬤⬤⬤⬤⬤⬤ 16

    56

×16

72

(i) How much money did Ulrika raise?   (1)

(ii) How much more did Will raise than Stella?   (2)

(iii) What is the total amount of money raised by the friends?   (3)

6.3 Marc has carried out a survey of the numbers of passengers in the cars which passed his gate during a one-hour period. He has drawn the graph below to show his results.

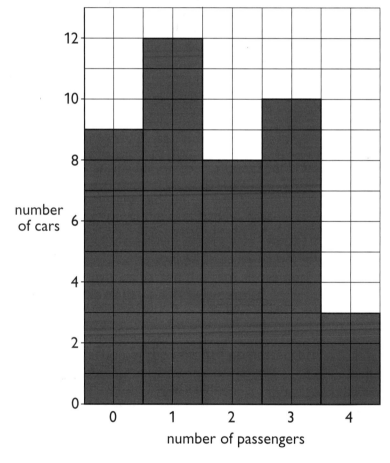

(i) How many cars had

    (a) no passengers   (1)

    (b) three or more passengers?   (1)

(ii) How many cars passed the gate altogether?   (2)

Remember that, in addition to the passengers, every car had a driver!

(iii) How many people passed the gate in cars?   (4)

(iv) What fraction of the cars had no passengers?   (2)

Grouping data into class intervals

AIM HIGH

- Suppose we have examination scores marked out of 100 rather than the five possible scores with the pentagonal spinner (see page 135).
- We *could*, of course, have 100 bars on a bar line graph or frequency diagram, but it is more practical to group the data into suitable **class intervals** such as

  0–9   10–19   20–29   30–39   and so on.

Interpreting data

Look at the following data concerning the scores out of 10 achieved by the twelve children.

Name	Score	Name	Score
Andy	8	George	4
Bea	7	Helen	8
Celia	5	Irene	8
David	6	June	10
Eddie	7	Kath	3
Fran	10	Lara	8

In ascending order, the scores are:

3   4   5   6   7   7   8   8   8   8   10   10

Range

The **range** of a set of raw data is the **difference** between the largest and smallest values. The range here is **7** (10 − 3).

Mode

The **mode** is the **most common** number. The mode here is **8** because there are more 8s than any other score.

Median

The **median** of a set of scores is the **middle** one when they are all arranged in order.

- To see how this works, look just at the five highest scores.   8   8   **8**   10   10
- The median of these five highest scores is 8 because 8 is the middle figure.
- If you look for the median of the whole group of twelve scores you will see that the number of scores is even. When this happens, you need to take the mean (see below) of the middle two scores. The mean of 7 and 8 is 7.5
- In other words, we find the value 'half way' between the two 'middle' numbers:

  3   4   5   6   7   **7   8**   8   8   8   10   10
  7.5

AIM HIGH

Mean

The mean of a set of scores is found by adding the scores and then dividing by the number of scores. In the example, the sum of the scores is 84 and there are twelve scores, so the mean is 7 (84 ÷ 12).

Representing continuous data

Line graphs

A line graph can show how something changes over time.

EXAMPLE 1:

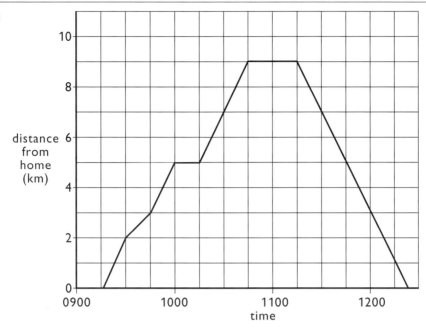

- This line graph (sometimes called a travel graph) shows Ben's distance from home when he cycled to his friend's house one day.

- How long did Ben spend at his friend's house?

EXAMPLE 2:

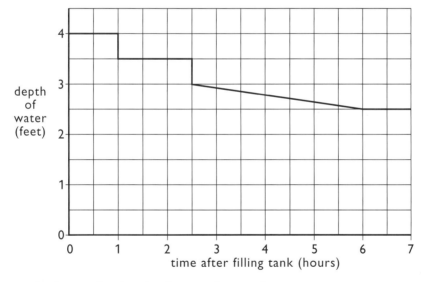

- This line graph shows the depth of water in a tank.

- At what times was water taken from the tank?

- For how long was the tap left dripping?

Conversion graphs

A conversion graph shows a fixed relationship between two **variables**.

AIM HIGH

EXAMPLE 1:

Metric to Imperial unit conversion

- This graph converts kilograms to pounds and vice versa.

- We need two reference points in order to draw the line, in this case (0, 0) and (1, 2.2) since we know that 1 kilogram is very nearly the same as 2.2 lb.

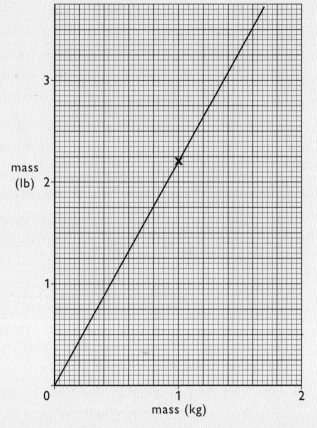

EXAMPLE 2:

Length of silver braid and cost in pounds

- A shopkeeper has bought a 25 metre roll of silver braid for £18.75.

- He intends to 'double his money' and get back £37.50 eventually, when he has sold all of the braid. His customers can buy any length of braid.

- This graph allows the shopkeeper to find the price for any length of silver braid he is asked for. The reference points are (0, 0) and (25, 37.5).

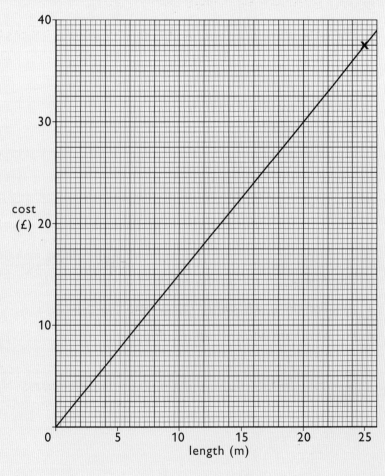

Using a conversion graph

Ask a number of people – such as your family, friends, teachers and neighbours – to tell you their mass.

Almost certainly, some will give the mass in kilograms and others will give the mass in stones and pounds. Remember that 1 stone is the same as 14 pounds.

Use the kilograms/pounds conversion graph on page 144 to prepare a table giving the masses of the people in both kilograms and pounds.

Questions

The answers are at the back of the book.

6.4 Andy bought a bag containing 200 coloured centimetre cubes.

He sorted them into groups of different colours and then drew the 'fraction diagram' below.

red	blue	yellow

(i)   What percentage of the cubes was red? (1)

(ii) What fraction, in its lowest terms, of the cubes was blue? (1)

(iii) How many cubes were yellow? (1)

(iv) Write down the ratio (in its simplest form) of the numbers of
      red cubes : blue cubes : yellow cubes (3)

6.5 Here are the numbers of hockey goals scored in a week by five children.

Anne	**Brian**	**Corrie**	**Diana**	**Edwina**
4	2	1	7	1

For these numbers, what is

(i)   the range (1)

(ii) the median (1)

(iii) the mode (1)

(iv) the mean?  (2)

6.6 The heights of the members of the McGregor family are 183 cm, 177 cm, 145 cm, 139 cm and 121 cm.

(i)   For the heights of the family members, what is

    (a) the range (1)

    (b) the median? (1)

(ii) What is the mean height of the family members? AIM HIGH (3)

6.7 The children in Miss Grant's class have made this list of their waist measurements in centimetres:

61	72	68	63	69
58	67	62	69	57
70	61	70	78	67
65	63	62	64	75

(i) From the raw data above, what is

    (a) the range (2)

    (b) the median? (3)

(ii) Copy and complete the table. (4)

Waist measurement (cm)	Tally marks	Frequency
55 to 57		
58 to 60		
61 to 63		
64 to 66		
67 to 69		
70 to 72		
73 to 75		
76 to 78		
Total		

(iii) Use the table to draw a frequency diagram. (3)

(iv) Which group of waist measurements is the mode? (1)

6.8 The line graph below shows the temperature inside Mr Christie's greenhouse, recorded every hour for 15 hours, one day in February.

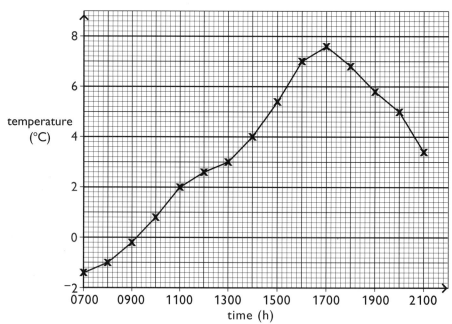

(i) What was the temperature at noon? (1)

(ii) At what time was the highest temperature recorded? (1)

(iii) Suggest values, during the 15-hour period, for

    (a) the range of temperatures (2)

    (b) the median recorded temperature. (3)

6.9 Use the conversion graph on page 144 to find out

    (i)   how much the shopkeeper would charge for a 2.5 metre length of silver braid   (2)

    (ii)   what length of silver braid a customer would receive if she asked for £5 worth.   (2)

HINT: If you are having trouble with question 6.9 you might try the following helpful hints: for part (i) find the cost of 10 metres first; for part (ii) find how much you could get for £15 first.

Multiple choice questions

In these questions you should write the letter of the correct answer.

6.10 What is the median of this set of data?   (1)

6	8	3	8	5	7	2	9	5	4	8

A: $4\frac{1}{2}$ B: 5   C: $5\frac{1}{2}$ D: 6   E: $6\frac{1}{2}$

6.11 The Carroll diagram below shows the results of a survey where the students in a year group were asked if they sang in the choir.

	choir	not choir
girl	17	9
boy	10	13

How many more girls than boys are there in the year group?   (1)

A: 3   B: 4   C: 6   D: 7   E: 8

6.2 PROBABILITY

Likelihood

The likelihood of an event happening may be

- **certain** — the event will always happen

EXAMPLE:	If you drop a coin into a bowl of water, the coin will sink.

- **likely** — the event will probably happen
- **even chance** — the event has a 'fifty-fifty' chance of happening

EXAMPLE:	If you toss a fair coin, you are equally likely to get 'heads' or 'tails'.

- **unlikely** — the event will probably *not* happen
- **impossible** — the event could never happen (no chance)

EXAMPLE:	If you roll an ordinary die, you will never get a 7

Life events

Think of examples of events in your life which are

- impossible
- very unlikely
- unlikely
- likely
- very likely
- certain

Outcomes of events

AIM HIGH

Before we can decide on the probability of an event happening, we need to know the number of possible, equally likely, **outcomes** of the event.

It is very useful to list these possible outcomes.

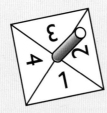
A

B

EXAMPLE 1: When a fair coin is tossed, there are just two possible outcomes, 'heads' and 'tails'.

EXAMPLE 2: With a square spinner, there are four possible outcomes.

With spinner A, the four outcomes are 1, 2, 3 and 4

With spinner B, the four outcomes are 'shaded', 'shaded', 'white' and 'shaded'.

EXAMPLE 3: With an ordinary *fair* die there are six possible outcomes.

The probability scale

The **probability scale** runs from **0** (no chance) to **1** (certain).

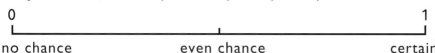

The **probability** of an event happening is usually expressed as a fraction.

> EXAMPLE 1: With a fair coin, the probability of getting 'heads' is $\frac{1}{2}$
>
> EXAMPLE 2: With spinner A (opposite), the probability of scoring 3 is $\frac{1}{4}$ because there is one section labelled '3' out of the four sections, and the probability of scoring an even number is $\frac{1}{2}$ because two of the four sections have even numbers.
>
> With spinner B (opposite), the probability of getting 'white' is $\frac{1}{4}$ and the probability of getting 'shaded' is $\frac{3}{4}$
>
> EXAMPLE 3: With a fair die, the probability of getting a four is $\frac{1}{6}$ and the probability of *not* getting a four is $\frac{5}{6}$

Sometimes, the probability of an event may be expressed in other ways. The probability of getting 'heads' with a fair coin could be expressed as 50%, 50 : 50 or 1 in 2

The **experimental** probability may not be the same as the **expected** (calculated) probability. If you toss a coin 100 times, you may not get 50 'heads' and 50 'tails'.

This may be because

- the number of trials is too low
- the coin may be **biased** (unfair).

Outcomes of two events at the same time

AIM HIGH

If two events are happening at the same time, then it is a very good idea to write all possible outcomes in a table. If you spin the two square spinners **A** and **B** at the same time, there are *sixteen* possible outcomes:

A	B	A	B	A	B	A	B
1	shaded	2	shaded	3	shaded	4	shaded
1	shaded	2	shaded	3	shaded	4	shaded
1	shaded	2	shaded	3	shaded	4	shaded
1	white	2	white	3	white	4	white

To do

Spinners

Make two pentagonal spinners like this.

Spinner **P** should be a perfect regular pentagon and spinner **Q** should be slightly irregular.

Spin each spinner 100 times and record your results.

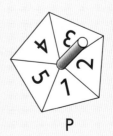

P

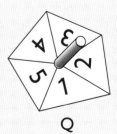

Q

Dice

Roll two ordinary dice at the same time and record the total score in a tally like the one shown below. You can decide how many times to roll them, but 100 times would be a good idea.

Total	Tally	Frequency
2		
3		
4		
5		
6		
7		
8		
9		
10		
11		
12		

Note that a total score of 1 is not possible!

Which totals seem to be the least likely and the most likely?

Complete a table of all possible outcomes like the one below.

		Second die				
		1	2	3	4	5	6
First die	1						
	2						
	3						
	4						
	5						
	6						

Probability experiments

Devise, and carry out, some probability experiments of your own. Here are some examples to give you ideas.

EXAMPLE 1: Investigate what happens when you drop a plastic farm animal, such as a pig.

First, find out the number of possible positions the pig could come to rest – perhaps on its

- feet
- back
- left side
- right side.

Now drop the pig 100 times and keep a tally of the number of times the pig comes to rest in each position.

If you don't have a plastic pig then you could use a plastic bottle top but this is not quite as much fun and there are really only three ways it could come to rest!

EXAMPLE 2:

You need a selection of buttons of different colours. Ask someone to put ten buttons (their choice of colours etc) in a bag.

You pull out a button at random and record the details. **Put the button back in the bag**.

The person shakes the bag and you pull out another button, again recording the details before replacing the button.

After doing this about 20 times, you should begin to have an idea about the colours of the buttons in the bag. When you think you know, ask for your prediction to be checked and gain a point for each correct prediction.

If the buttons are not all exactly the same size, the task is easier. For example, you might record

- red, large, two holes   for one button, and
- red, small, four holes   for another.

That way, you can be more confident that you have not picked the same button twice!

Questions

The answers are at the back of the book.

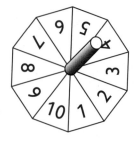

6.12 Pedro is using this spinner in a game.

Choose your answers from the following:

impossible   very unlikely   unlikely   even chance

likely   very likely   certain

Choose from the options above, the one which best describes the probability of scoring:

(i) 5   (1)

(ii) an odd number   (1)

(iii) a prime number   (2)

(iv) a number smaller than 7   (1)

(v) a common multiple of 3 and 4   (1)

6.13 Joanne has an ordinary coin and a pentagonal spinner.

(i)   How many possible outcomes are there
      when Joanne

   (a) tosses the coin   (1)

   (b) spins the spinner?   (1)

(ii) Next Joanne tosses the coin and spins the spinner at the same time. One possible
      outcome is T (tails) and A. List all the possible outcomes.   (4)

6.14 Graham has two ordinary dice, one white and one grey.

He rolls the dice at the same time.

(i)   Describe all the ways it is possible to score a total of

   (a) 4   (2)

   (b) 10   (3)

Using these two dice, Graham plays a game with his friends. To start, the player must get a
score of 10

Graham says that this is more likely than rolling two sixes.

(ii) Is he right? Explain your answer.   (2)

6.15 Peter has the following items:

Copy the probability scales, and mark with a cross the probabilities of the events.

W

(i) When the spinner is spun, the score will be 3 (1)

0   1

(ii) When the coin is tossed, it will land showing tails or heads. (1)

0   1

(iii) When the die is rolled, it will show an odd prime number. (1)

0   1

6.16 Penelope has written the letters of her name on cards.

| P | E | N | E | L | O | P | E |

Penelope shuffles the cards and takes one card at random.

What is the probability that the letter on the card is

(i) a vowel (1)

(ii) P (1)

(iii) E (2)

(iv) a letter with reflection symmetry? (1)

Multiple choice questions

In these questions you should write the letter of the correct answer.

6.17 How many of these events have a probability of $\frac{1}{2}$? (1)

(a) You get heads when a fair coin is tossed.

(b) You get a 4 when an octagonal spinner numbered 1, 2, 3, 4, 5, 6, 7, 8 is spun.

(c) You get a letter N if you choose a card at random from a set with the letters of Anne's name.

| A | N | N | E |

(d) You get an even number when a fair die is rolled.

(e) You get a shape with rotation symmetry if you choose a card at random from a set of cards with these names:

square   rhombus   scalene triangle   kite

parallelogram   isosceles triangle

(f) You get a prime number when an ordinary die is rolled.

A: **1**   B: **2**   C: **3**   D: **4**   E: **5**

6.18 Which of these events does *not* have a probability of $\frac{1}{3}$? (1)

A: You get a multiple of 3 when an ordinary die is rolled.

B: You get an even number when a triangular spinner numbered 1, 2, 3 is spun.

C: You get the shortest straw when you are the first to draw from 3 straws.

D: You get a 2 when an ordinary fair die is rolled.

E: You get a square number when an ordinary die is rolled.

APPENDIX 1 MAKING A MICROBALANCE

Introduction

A microbalance can be used to find the mass of a small object, such as a grain of sand.

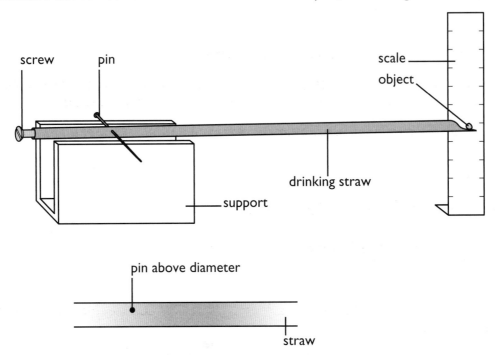

A traditional microbalance looks something like the one shown in the diagram above.

With a microbalance we compare the unknown mass (for example a grain of sand) with known masses (usually made from graph paper).

Making a simple microbalance

To make the one shown here, you will need:

- a drinking straw (ideally a plastic one)
- a long, thin pin (or needle)
- a metal bolt (or screw), of length between 1 cm and 2 cm, which will screw fairly tightly into the end of the straw
- a sheet of graph paper
- a matchbox or something similar to make a support
- a scale.

METHOD

1. Cut two short (4 mm) parallel slits in one end of the straw and carefully push in the flap with a pencil. This gives a little 'tray' at the end of the straw.

2. Carefully screw the bolt into the other end of the straw.

3. Push the pin through the straw, at right angles, above the diameter, about 2 cm from the bolt end.

4. Rest the pin on the support and screw the bolt in or out until the straw balances in a roughly horizontal position.

Don't worry if you can't achieve this first time. Straws and bolts vary, so you may need to adjust the position of the pin along the straw slightly.

Making small standard masses ('weights')

Standard graph paper has a mass of about 80 grams per square metre.

This means that the mass of a one centimetre square is about 0.008 gram (8 thousandths of a gram or 8 milligrams).

METHOD

1. Cut a one centimetre square from a sheet of graph paper.

2. From this centimetre square cut five strips, each 10 mm long and 2 mm wide. Each of these strips has a mass of about 0.0016 gram (1.6 milligram). Keep two of these strips.

3. Cut another strip into two halves. Each of these pieces will have a mass of about 0.0008 gram (0.8 milligrams).

4. Make a few smaller standard masses.

You could make other standard masses if you need them.

Measuring the mass of a small object

METHOD

1. Set up your microbalance with the straw in a roughly horizontal position. Note the position of the tray in relation to the scale.

2. Very carefully place a small object such as a grain of sand, on the tray at the end of the straw.

   The straw will dip below its original position.

3. Make a note of the new position on the scale.

4. Carefully remove the object and then add standard masses until the straw reaches the position that you noted in step 3.

5. Calculate the mass of the object by adding up the values of the masses you added in step 4.

APPENDIX 2 PROGRAMMING IN BBC BASIC

Introduction

Computers are now an essential part of life for most of us and we use them in many ways. Modern computers are increasingly complex and we generally make use of the programs written by skilled, professional programmers.

In the 1980s computers in schools and homes were much simpler (and more limited) and many people gained a great deal of satisfaction from writing and using their own programs.

You may have access to an old BBC computer, but it is assumed here that you will be using a PC.

An excellent version of BBC BASIC is available as a free download from **R.T. Russell The Home of BBC BASIC** (www.cix.co.uk/~rrussell).

If you download BBC BASIC you can use it in the following ways.

Programs to practise basic mathematical skills

Multiplication tables

Type in the program below, exactly as shown.

```
10   REM PRACTISING MULTIPLICATION TABLES
20   LET E=0
30   PRINT "Enter difficulty level (1 to 5)"
40   INPUT D
50   IF D<1 OR D>5 THEN GOTO 30
60   TIME=0
70   FOR Q=1 TO 10
80   CLS
90   LET X=RND(D+7)
100  LET Y=RND(D+7)
120  PRINT "Question ";Q
130  PRINT "Multiply ";X;" by ";Y;" and enter your answer."
150  LET Z=X*Y
170  INPUT A
190  IF A<>Z THEN GOTO 240
200  PRINT "You have taken ";TIME/100;" seconds"
210  PRINT "You have made ";E;" errors"
220  NEXT Q
230  STOP
240  PRINT "No. Try again"
250  LET E=E+1
260  GOTO 170
```

The highlighted words are keywords in BBC BASIC.

Ignore the fact that line numbers 110, 140, 160 and 180 seem to be missing. The reason for this will become clear later!

Type RUN and all should be well.

If there is an error, then check and try again.

The following notes will help you to understand how the program works.

- The keyword REM in line 10 is a **remark** and plays no part when you RUN the program.

- The **variable** E (set to zero in line 20 and updated in line 250) counts the number of errors.

- In line 60, the variable TIME is set to zero. When the program is run, the computer keeps a record of the time taken.

- The keyword CLS in line 80 clears the screen.

- The '<>' in line 190 means 'not equal to'.

- The FOR...NEXT loop (lines 70 to 220) sets and asks ten questions and checks your answers, moving straight on to the next question (line 220) unless you make an error, when you are asked to try again (and maybe again!) until you enter the correct answer (lines 240 to 260).

Division with a remainder

The program below will provide practice with carrying out divisions with a remainder.

Type in the program exactly as it appears here. Alternatively you could simply modify the first program since many of the lines are the same. This is why some line numbers were missing in the first program!

Be careful to check where this listing differs from the first one.

```
10    REM PRACTISING DIVISION WITH A REMAINDER
20    LET E=0
30    PRINT "Enter difficulty level (1 to 5)"
40    INPUT D
50    IF D<1 OR D>5 THEN GOTO 30
60    TIME=0
70    FOR Q=1 TO 10
80    CLS
90    LET X=(D+5)*RND(20)
100   LET Y=D+RND(7)
110   IF Y>=X THEN GOTO 80
120   PRINT "Question ";Q
130   PRINT " Divide ";X;" by ";Y
140   PRINT "Enter the number of times ";Y;" goes into ";X;" then the remainder"
150   LET S=X DIV Y
160   LET R=X MOD Y
170   INPUT A
180   INPUT B
190   IF A<>S OR B<>R THEN GOTO 240
200   PRINT "You have taken ";TIME/100;" seconds"
210   PRINT "You have made ";E;" errors"
220   NEXT Q
```

```
230   STOP
240   PRINT "No. Try again"
250   LET E=E+1
260   GOTO 170
```

You will notice that a few new things are introduced in this program. For example:

- The '>=' in line 110 means 'greater than or equal to' and this line checks to make sure that the number you are dividing by is the smaller of the two.

Once the program is running, you could use it in a competition with your friends – with everyone entering the same level of difficulty to be fair!

A few suggestions

You might like to write a program, or modify one of the two here, to practise using

- addition facts

- subtraction facts

- multiplication facts other than tables – for example any two-digit number multiplied by any single-digit number.

The possibilities are endless. Now it is over to you!

APPENDIX 3 SHAPES DOMINOES

Here is a set of shapes dominoes for you to photocopy and use.

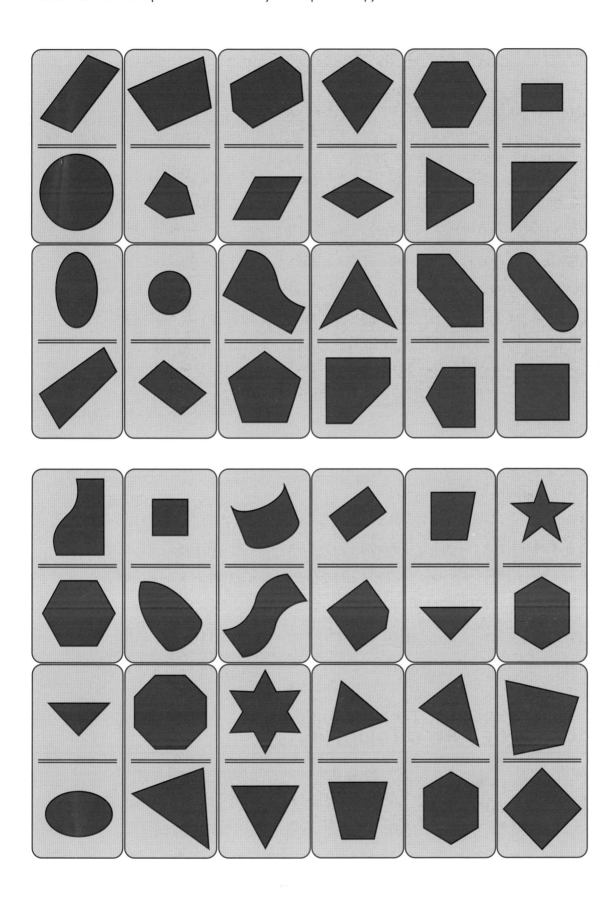

ANSWERS

1 NUMBER

1.1 PROPERTIES OF NUMBERS

1.1 (i) 3   (2)

(ii) square number   (1)

(iii) (a) 12   (1)   (b) 6   (1)   (c) 27   (1)

1.2 (i) 11 (1)   (ii) 3   (1)   (iii) 28   (1)

(iv) 2   (1)   (v) ⁻9   (1)   (vi) 9   (1)

(vii) ⁻6 (1)   (viii) 2 remainder 2   (1)

1.3 (i) 17 °C   (1)   (ii) 15 °C   (2)

1.4 (i) 26, 31, 36   (1)   (ii) 12, 5, ⁻2   (2)   (iii) 5.0, 5.2, 5.4   (2)

1.5 (i) 51, 59   (1)   (ii) 65, 58   (1)   (iii) 0, ⁻3   (2)

1.6 (i) 21, 34   (2)   (ii) 36, 49   (1)   (iii) 72, 98   (2)

1.7 (a) Factor rainbow for 48 drawn.   (4)

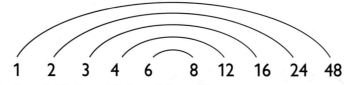

1   2   3   4   6   8   12   16   24   48

(b) 1 and 18, 2 and 9, 3 and 6   (2)

1.8 (i) 35   (1)   (ii) 5   (1)   (iii) 4   (1)

(iv) 5 and 11   (2)   (v) 24   (1)   (vi) 15   (1)

(vii) 4 and 12   (1)   (viii) 15 and 24 or 24 and 33 (1)

(ix) 5, 15 and 35 or 4, 24 and 27 (2)   (x) 27   (1)

1.9 C   (1)   **1.10** C   (1)   **1.11** B   (1)

1.12 D   (1)   **1.13** D   (1)   **1.14** D   (1)

1.15 E   (1)

1.2 PLACE VALUE AND ORDERING

1.16 (i) 6020   (1)   (ii) forty thousand, four hundred and four (1)

1.17 (i) 5 tens (50)   (1)   (ii) 9 thousands (9000) (1) (iii) 1000 times (2)

1.18 43.7   89.71   0.75   (3)

1.19 (i) 40 600   (1)   (ii) 3.05   (1)   (iii) 29.5   (1)

(iv) 30.4   (1)   (v) 3.05   (1)

1.20 (i) 100 times (1)   (ii) 1000 times (1)   (iii) 10 000 times (1)

       (iv) 1000 times (1)   (v) 100 000 times (1)

1.21 (i) 5 marked (1)

       (ii) 0.6 marked (1)

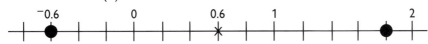

       (iii) $2\frac{1}{4}$ marked (1)

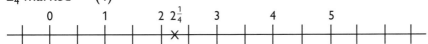

1.22 (i) integers $x < 2$ circled (2)

       (ii) integers $y \geq {}^{-}1$ circled (2)

1.23 (i) 679, 697, 769, 796, 967 (2)   (ii) 5.34, 4.53, 4.35, 3.54, 3.45 (2)

1.24 C (1)   **1.25** D (1)   **1.26** A (1)

1.3 ESTIMATION AND APPROXIMATION

1.27 (i) 4 marked (1)

       (ii) 70 marked (1)

1.28 (i) 16 000 (1)   (ii) 80 (1)

1.29 20 hours (3)

1.30 (i) 490 (1)   (ii) 800 (1)   (iii) 3 (1)

1.31 B (1)   **1.32** B (1)   **1.33** E (1)

1.4 FRACTIONS, DECIMALS, PERCENTAGES AND RATIO

1.34 fraction strip showing $\frac{5}{7}$ drawn (2)

1.35 36 kg (2)   **1.36** 84 mm (2)

1.37 (i) $\frac{1}{11}$ (1)   (ii) $\frac{7}{10}$ (1)

1.38 (i)   diagram completed   (2)

equivalent fraction machine

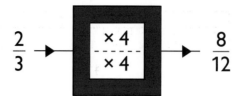

(ii)   diagram completed   (2)

simplest form machine

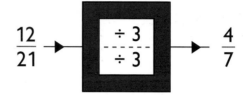

1.39 £20   (2)

1.40 table completed   (9)

Fraction (in simplest form)	$\frac{2}{5}$	$\frac{1}{4}$	$\frac{7}{20}$	$\frac{4}{5}$	$\frac{7}{10}$
Decimal	0.4	0.25	0.35	0.8	0.7
Percentage	40%	25%	35%	80%	70%

1.41 (i)   7 : 3   (2)   (ii)   7 : 10   (2)

1.42 (i)   (a)   8   (1)   (b)   18   (1)

      (ii)   20 chocolates, 16 mints   (2)

1.43 80 : 100 : 120   (3)

1.44 A   (1)   **1.45** D   (1)   **1.46** E   (1)

2 CALCULATIONS

2.1 NUMBER OPERATIONS

2.1   7 + 13 = 20 shown   (1)

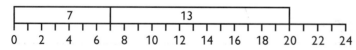

2.2   17 − 8 = 9 shown   (1)

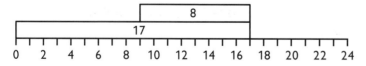

2.3   5 × 3 = 15 shown   (1)

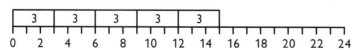

2.4   21 ÷ 7 = 3 shown   (1)

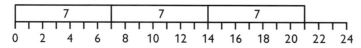

2.5 23 ÷ 6 → 3 remainder 5 shown   (1)

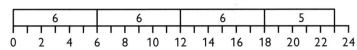

2.6 24 + 17 = 41   41 − 17 = 24   41 − 24 = 17   (3)

2.7 7 × 13 = 91   91 ÷ 7 = 13   91 ÷ 13 = 7   (3)

2.8 C   (1)   **2.9** E   (1)

2.2 MENTAL STRATEGIES

2.10 (i) 87   (1)   (ii) 204   (1)   (iii) 495   (1)

2.11 (i) 36   (1)   (ii) 23   (1)

2.12 267 chickens   (1)   **2.13** 36 people   (1)   **2.14** £9.88   (1)

2.15 08:40   (1)   **2.16** 72   (1)

2.17 (i) 160   (1)   (ii) 1.6   (1)   (iii) 1.6   (1)

(iv) 0.8   (1)

2.18 C   (1)   **2.19** C   (1)

2.3 WRITTEN METHODS

For questions 2.20 to 2.25 full working is expected.

2.20 (a) 180   (1)   (b) 77   (2)

2.21 (a) 12.6   (1)   (b) 11.02   (2)

2.22 (a) 6.7   (1)   (b) 11.8   (2)

2.23 (a) 152   (2)   (b) 6384   (2)

2.24 (a) 409   (2)   (b) 286   (2)

2.25 (a) £43.75   (2)

(b) (i) £5.71   (2)   (ii) 3 pence   (2)

2.26 D   (1)   **2.27** D   (1)

2.4 CALCULATOR METHODS

2.28 (i) the answer must be odd, because odd ÷ odd is always odd;

the units digit must be 7 since only a number ending in 7 gives a number ending in 1 when multiplied by 3 (2)

(ii) 17   (1)

2.29 £2.89   (3)   **2.30** B   (1)   **2.31** E   (1)

3 PROBLEM SOLVING

3.2 REASONING ABOUT NUMBERS OR SHAPES

3.1 37 and 61   (2)

3.2 (i)   £1, 20p, 20p and 10p   (1)   (ii)   2p and 1p   (2)

3.3 47 (2 less than 49)   (3)

3.4 18 (Connor's numbers are 6 and 12)   (3)

3.5 (i)   (a) Q   (1)   (b) P   (1)   (c) R   (1)

     (ii)   (a) S drawn   (1)   (b) T drawn   (1)

        S   T   U   V

     (c) U drawn   (1)   (d) V drawn   (2)

3.6 five shapes drawn   (5)

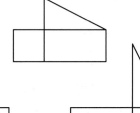
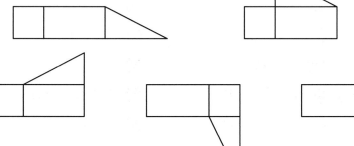

3.3 REAL-LIFE MATHEMATICS

3.7 £2.53   (3)

3.8 (i)   25.5%   (1)   (ii)   20 g   (3)   (iii)   12.6 g   (2)

3.9 9 pence   (3)

3.10 (i)   table completed   (4)

	to make 6 scones	to make 24 scones
butter	50 g	200 g
flour	225 g	900 g
baking powder	3 tsp	12 tsp
salt	$\frac{1}{2}$ tsp	2 tsp
caster sugar	30 g	120 g
sultanas	50 g	200 g
milk	150 ml	600 ml
eggs	1	4

preparation time 10 minutes

cooking time 15 minutes

     (ii)   15 minutes!   (1)

3.11 (i) 12 minutes 31 seconds   (2)

(ii) team B   (4)
(team A total time 12 hours 56 minutes 22 seconds
team B total time 12 hours 48 minutes 45 seconds)

3.12 (i) (a) $\frac{1}{5}$ (2)   (b) 38%   (2)   (c) 2 : 1   (2)

(ii) 50 p   (2)   (iii) £35 (he made £10 profit)   (2)

(iv) It is more likely that a green duck will win, but it is the number on the duck that is important and every duck has an equal chance of winning!   (2)

(v) (a) £8   (1)   (b) £2   (2)

(vi) $\frac{4}{5}$ (2)

(vii) (a) $\frac{9}{50}$ (2)   (b) $\frac{3}{10}$ (3)

4 ALGEBRA

4.1 EQUATIONS AND FORMULAE

4.1 (i) 15 years   (1)   (ii) 7 cm   (1)

4.2 (a) (i) 16   (1)   (ii) 15   (1)   (iii) 4   (1)

(iv) 4   (1)   (v) 9   (2)

(b) (i) $a = 7$ (1)   (ii) $b = 12$ (1)   (iii) $c = 5$ (1)

(iv) $d = 2$ (2)   (v) $e = 7$ (3)

4.3 (a) 12   (1)   (b) 14   (1)   (c) 9   (1)

(d) 35   (1)

(e) (i) $7k + 6$ (1)   (ii) 41   (1)

(f) (i) $3(j + 4)$ (1)   (ii) 30   (1)

(g) (i) $a + b + c$ (1)   (ii) 14   (1)

4.2 SEQUENCES AND FUNCTIONS

4.4 (i) (a) 6   (1)   (b) 13   (1)

(ii) 0   (2)

4.5 (i) (a) 4   (1)   (b) 16   (1)

(ii) 1   (2)

4.6 (a) 7   (2)   (b) 3   (2)

4.7 (i) (a) + 3 (b) 18, 21   (1)   (ii) (a) × 2 (b) 32, 64   (1)

(iii) (a) − 4 (b) 17, 13   (2)   (iv) (a) − 3 (b) 0, ‾3   (2)

4.8 (i) 22, 29   (2)   (ii) 29, 47   (2)

4.9 × 2, × 3 and × 6   (2)

4.10 (i) arrangement 4 sketched   (1)

arrangement 4

    (ii) (a) 16 straws   (1)   (b) 25 straws   (2)

    (iii) yes   (1)   (iv) function machine drawn   (3)

    (v) (a) 301 straws   (1)   (b) 3001 straws   (1)

    (vi) arrangement 333 333   (2)

4.3 GRAPHS

4.11 (i) table of outputs completed   (2)

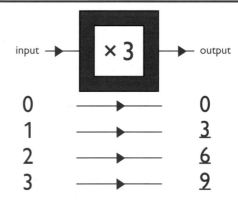

    (ii) points plotted on grid   (2)

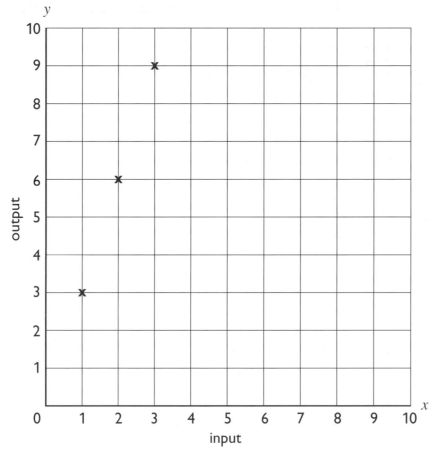

4.12 (i) 1   (1)   (ii) 3   (1)

    (iii) output = input − 1   (2)

4.13 (i)　points plotted on grid　　(2)

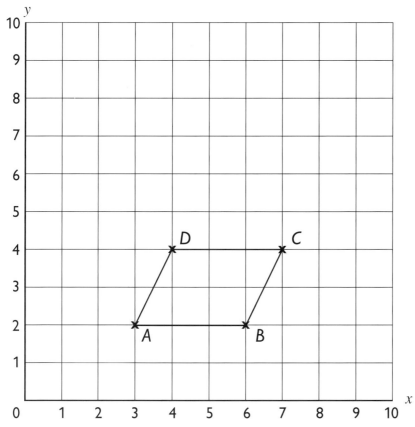

(ii)　*ABCD* drawn　(2)　　　　(iii)　parallelogram　(1)　　(iv)　(5, 3)　(1)

4.14 (i)　(a)　(0, 3), (1, 4), (2, 5), (3, 6), (4, 7)　(2)　　　(b)　points plotted on grid　(2)

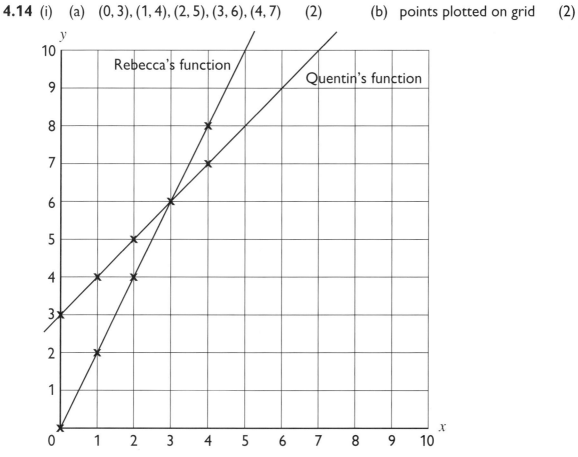

(c)　graph drawn and labelled　(1)

(ii)　(a)　(0, 0), (1, 2), (2, 4), (3, 6), (4, 8)　(2)

(b)　points plotted on grid　(2)　　　　　(c)　graph drawn and labelled　(1)

4.15 diagram completed   (3)

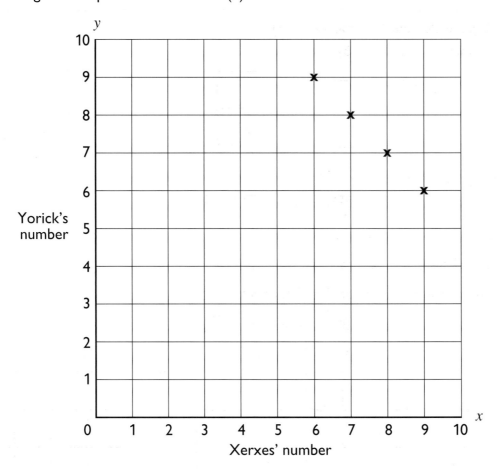

Possibilities: 9 and 6   8 and 7   7 and 8   6 and 9

5 SHAPE, SPACE AND MEASURES

5.1 MEASURES

5.1 (a) (i) 305 cm   (1)   (ii) 3050 mm   (1)   (iii) 10 ft 2 inches   (2)

      (b) (i) 45 000 g   (1)   (ii) 99 lb   (2)   (iii) 7 stones 1 lb   (1)

5.2 (i) 28 cm   (1)   (ii) 48 cm²   (1)

5.3 (i) 5 cm³   (2)   (ii) 7 cm³   (2)   (iii) 9 cm³   (2)

5.4 (a) (i) 13:09   (1)   (ii) 06:45   (1)

      (b) (i) 6.36 pm   (1)   (ii) 8.15 pm   (1)

5.5 (i) 1.5   (1)   (ii) 0.85   (1)

      (iii) 6.5   (2)   (iv) 2.5   (2)

5.6 C   (1)   **5.7** E   (1)   **5.8** C   (1)

5.2 SHAPE

5.9 (i) A kite, B parallelogram, C rectangle   (3)

(ii) lines of symmetry drawn   (3)

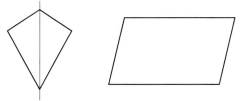

(iii) rotation symmetry described   (2)

kite   no rotation symmetry (order 1)
parallelogram   order 2
rectangle   order 2

5.10 (i) sketch of right-angled isosceles triangle   (2)

(ii) 'are *all* angles the same?' or suitable alternative   (2)

5.11 (i) S   (1)   (ii) Q, R and U   (3)

5.12 (i) net drawn, for example as shown below   (3)

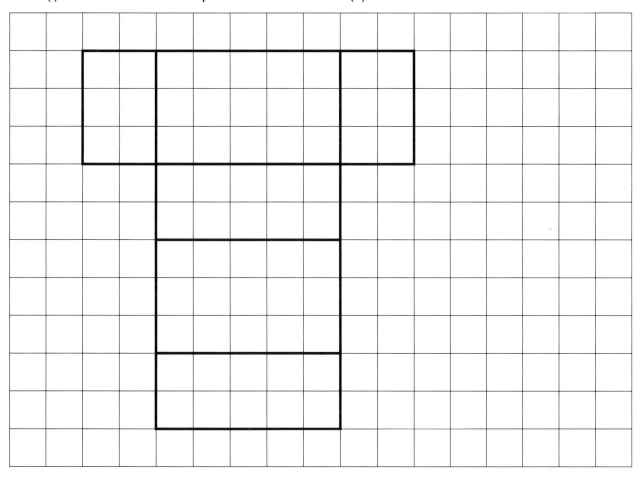

(ii) 30 cm³   (2)   (iii) 62 cm²   (3)

5.13 C   (1)   **5.14** D   (1)   **5.15** B   (1)

5.3 SPACE

5.16 (i) acute   about 30°   (2)   (ii) obtuse   about 100° to 110°   (2)

(iii) reflex   about 200°   (2)   (iv) reflex   about 300°   (2)

5.17 (a) (i) angle A: 70°   angle B: 44°   angle C: 66° (3)   (ii) 180° (1)

     (b) (i) (a) right angle (1)   (b) acute angle (1)

        (ii) right-angled scalene triangle (1)

5.18 a 130° (1) b 66° (1) c 66° (1)

     d 60° (1) e 110° (1) f 70° (1)

5.19 (i) east (2)   (ii) north-west (2)   (iii) north-east (2)

     (iv) north-west (2)   (v) north (2)

5.20 shape reflected in line *m* (3)

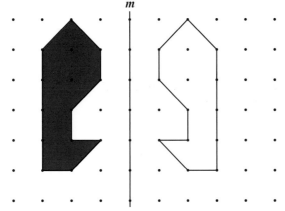

5.21 (i) Q drawn (2)   (ii) R drawn (2)   (iii) S drawn (2)

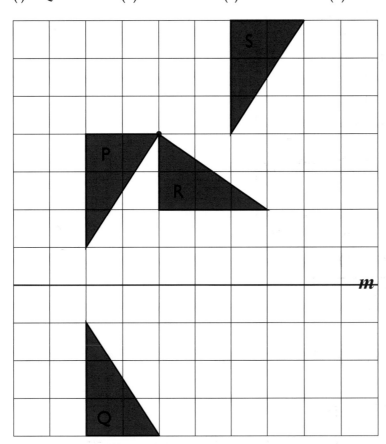

5.22 (i)   triangle constructed   (3)   (ii)   angle *ACB* is 79°   (1)

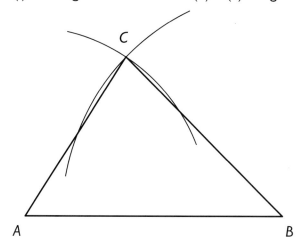

5.23 E   (1)   **5.24** B   (1)   **5.25** E   (1)

5.26 C   (1)   **5.27** C   (1)

6 HANDLING DATA

6.1 DATA HANDLING

6.1 (i)   Carroll diagram completed   (5)

	multiple of 3	not multiple of 3
not multiple of 7	12 54 6 36	13
multiple of 7	21 42	28 49 14

(ii)   Venn diagram completed   (5)

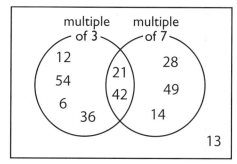

(iii) (a) range 48   (1)   (b) median 24.5   (2)   (c) mean 27.5   (2)

6.2 (i) £13   (1)   (ii) £7   (2)   (iii) £72   (3)

6.3 (i) (a) 9   (1)   (b) 13   (1)   (ii) 42   (2)

(iii) 112 (70 passengers and 42 drivers)   (4)   (iv) $\frac{3}{14}$ (2)

6.4 (i) 25%   (1)   (ii) $\frac{2}{5}$ (1)

(iii) 70   (1)   (iv) 5 : 8 : 7   (3)

6.5 (i) 6   (1)   (ii) 2   (1)

(iii) 1   (1)   (iv) 3   (2)

6.6 (i) (a) range 62 cm   (1)   (b) median 145 cm   (1)

(ii) 153 cm   (3)

6.7 (i) (a) 21 cm   (2)   (b) 66 cm (mean of 65 and 67)   (3)

(ii) table completed   (4)

Waist measurement (cm)	Tally marks	Frequency
55 to 57	/	1
58 to 60	/	1
61 to 63	## /	6
64 to 66	//	2
67 to 69	##	5
70 to 72	///	3
73 to 75	/	1
76 to 78	/	1
Total		20

(iii) frequency diagram drawn   (3)

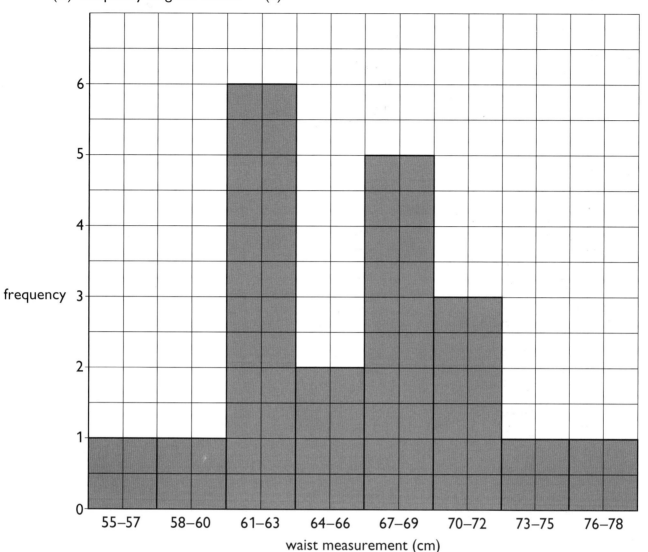

(iv) 61–63 cm   (1)

6.8 (i) 2.6 °C   (1)   (ii) 17:00 (the temperature was about 7.6 °C)   (1)

(iii) (a) 9.0 degrees (7.6 − ⁻1.4)   (2)   (b) 3.4 °C   (3)

6.9 (i) £3.75   (2)   (ii) 3.3 m or $3\frac{1}{3}$ m   (2)

6.10 D   (1)   **6.11** A   (1)

6.2 PROBABILITY

6.12 (i) very unlikely ($\frac{1}{10}$)   (1)   (ii) even chance ($\frac{1}{2}$)   (1)

(iii) unlikely ($\frac{2}{5}$)   (2)   (iv) likely ($\frac{3}{5}$)   (1)

(v) impossible (0)   (1)

6.13 (i) (a) 2   (1)   (b) 5   (1)

(ii) T A   H A
      T B   H B
      T C   H C
      T D   H D
      T E   H E   (4)

6.14 (i) (a)   1 and 3   2 and 2   3 and 1   (2)

            (b)   4 and 6   5 and 5   6 and 4   (3)

      (ii)   yes; three possibilities for 10 (4 and 6, 5 and 5, 6 and 4), but only one possibility for 12
(6 and 6)   (2)

6.15 (i) $\frac{2}{5}$ marked on probability scale   (1)

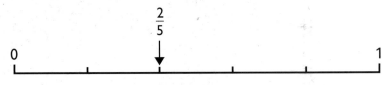

      (ii) $\frac{1}{2}$ marked   (1)

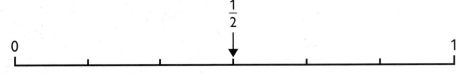

      (iii) $\frac{1}{3}$ marked   (1)

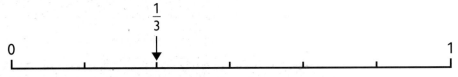

6.16 (i) $\frac{1}{2}$ (1)   (ii) $\frac{1}{4}$ (1)

       (iii) $\frac{3}{8}$ (1)   (iv) $\frac{1}{2}$ (1)

6.17 E   (1)   **6.18** D   (1)